Realising the Dream

The History of the Northern Racing College

1984-2007

John Cornwell

Published by South Yorkshire Training Trust
The Stables,
Rossington Hall,
Great North Road,
Doncaster DN 11 0HN
South Yorkshire.

SYTT Tel. No. 01302 861000
SYTT e-mail address is: info@northernracingcollege.co.uk

First Edition published September 2007

ISBN number: 978-0-9556698-0-4

Printed by Sheaf Graphics
Milton Street,
Sheffield S3 7WL

Other books by the author include:

"Against the Odds", the History of Sheffield Eagles RLFC 1984-94

Sheffield Eagles 1984-98 (Tempus Series)

"King Teds", the History of King Edward VII School, Sheffield

"Tomb of the Unknown Alderman", Tales from Sheffield City Council

"Pull Yourself Together!", Tales and Poems from two Yorkshire cities

Foreword

by the

Duke of Devonshire CBE

I followed closely the progress of the Northern Racing College during my chairmanship of the British Horseracing Board, since one of our responsibilities was training and education within the industry, and I was honoured and delighted to accept the role of President of the College in 2005.

I was extremely flattered to be asked to follow the Earl of Scarborough, the only previous President, because he made an enormous contribution to the College, albeit very much behind the scenes.

The Northern Racing College has done, and continues to do excellent work within the field of training for the British horseracing and breeding industries, and it can be proud of its history and achievements over the last twenty-three years.

Author's Preface

I had not been back to Rossington Hall for two decades when I was asked to write the history of the Northern Racing College. All I remembered was a small operation in the corner of the Victorian Stables run by the South Yorkshire County Council. It was one of their numerous projects to try and breathe some life back into the devastated economy of area. That was in the middle Eighties, when times were grim in our part of the world, and there was no certainty that any of our schemes would stay the course. Quite frankly, the training school seemed a bit of a luxury and one of the projects that seemed less likely to survive.

My only connection with the NRC was through my membership of the South Yorkshire County Council over two decades ago. However, as I researched the history of the College for this book, I was impressed time and again by the sheer determination, resilience and resourcefulness of the Trustees and Staff during those intervening years. The founders of the NRC stood the institution on its legs and then nurtured and developed it, so that recently it has won the highest awards possible for any type of training institution in the U.K. Those "founding fathers" were all part of the South Yorkshire County Council, either as councillors, such as Colin Wedd, who has been the Chair throughout the NRC's history, Roy Thwaites, the SYCC Leader, who gave the idea wings and was the Vice-Chair until 2004, and Jim Gale, who has been the professional head of the College since he was handed the brief in 1982, because his wife was a horse rider and therefore he might have an interest in the project.

As I have only been on a horse twice in my life, both embarrassing and even painful experiences, and have rarely been to a race meeting, I was very dependent on others for information about the College and the industry. On the positive side, I did have the fullest access to most of the people who have made the biggest contribution to the College over the last quarter of a century. I had long rigorous sessions with Jim Gale, who had the most amazing recall of facts and events since 1982, and also numerous illuminating discussions with Colin Wedd. Their support has been invaluable and they both gave me a Board perspective of why decisions were taken, and who were the key players in sustaining the NRC over the years.

When writing the history of any institution you are mindful of a number of different audiences. There are those who will want to know the "political" history of how the NRC survived and sustained itself over the years, while others will want to read about the "family" history of staff and trainees who have passed through Rossington Hall since 1984. I also felt it was imperative that this book served as a formal record of decisions taken and events experienced, even if sometimes they may seem a little tedious to the general reader.

May I also thank Michael Lindley, the son of Harry Lindley, and Gordon Blackwell for their information about the earliest days, when the idea of a racing training college was just a dream. I also appreciated the help of Ruth Harmon of Sheffield City Archives, who dug out a lot of information about the period 1982-86 from the South Yorkshire County Council archives, which are still unclassified and lying around in boxes at the archives in central Sheffield.

Paul Foster, Zoe Horne and Ben Mico, and several other members of the NRC's staff, helped to fill in the vast number of gaps in my knowledge of the College and put up with my numerous requests for photos and information. Dr. Peter Beeley, an Emeritus Fellow of Leeds University, once again kindly agreed to proof read one of my books, as did Patricia Waugh who also made some useful suggestions for the text. My thanks are also due to the Editor of the Star newspaper in Sheffield, and to the Yorkshire Post, for the use of a number of photographs in the book. Finally, I would like to thank Jenny Sayles and Terry Cooper of Sheaf Graphics for the superb job they have done laying out and printing the book.

J.C.Cornwell
Nether Edge, Sheffield

August 2007

Contents

Glossary

ALI	Adult Learning Inspectorate	MSC	Manpower Services Commission
AMA	Association of the Metropolitan Authorities	NRC	Northern Racing College (since 1995)
ABRS	Association of British Riding Schools.	NRS	Northern Racing School (1990-1995)
ARTS	Apprentice Racing Training School (1988-90)	NTF	National Trainers' Federation
ATO	Approved Training Organisation	NTP	National Training Partnership
BHB	British Horseracing Board	NVQ	National Vocational Qualification
BHEST	British Horseracing Education and Standards Trust	PRT	Programme Review Team
BHS	British Horse Society	QAO	Quality Assurance Officer
BSJA	British Show Jumping Association	RACE	Racing Academy and Centre of Education (Ireland)
BME	Black and Minority Ethnic	RHKJC	Royal Hong Kong Jockey Club
BRS	British Racing School	ROA	Racehorse Owners Association
DCVS	Doncaster Community Voluntary Service	RTBTB	Racing and Thoroughbred Training Board
DfES	Department for Education and Skills	SYARTS	South Yorkshire Apprentice Racing Training School (1984-88)
DMBC	Doncaster Metropolitan Borough Council	SYCC	South Yorkshire County Council (1973-86)
EARS	European Association of Racing Schools	SYTT	South Yorkshire Training Trust (1986 to the present)
EQUES	European Qualification for Employees in Stables	TBA	Thoroughbred Breeders' Association
HRLB	Horse Race Levy Board	TEC	Training and Enterprise Council
JNHETC	Joint National Horse Education and Training Council	TGWU	Transport and General Workers Union
IiP	Investors in People	YTS	Youth Training Scheme
LSC	Learning and Skills Council		

Harry's Legacy

Every successful institution, whether supranational or just important locally, starts with a single individual's bright idea. For twenty-five years all those involved with the Northern Racing College thought the dream of a training school to prepare young people to enter the horseracing industry was solely that of Harry Lindley. Recently, it has come to light that Gordon Blackwell may have had the dream first and passed on the idea to Harry, whose perseverance saw it turned into reality. Gordon Blackwell, originally from Leeds, was involved in horseracing in the USA in the late Sixties, and it was while he was there that he realised the importance of training youngsters for the different jobs needed in the racing industry. He returned to Britain in the early Seventies and a few years later conceived the idea of a racing training school. In 1979 he approached Doncaster Metropolitan Borough Council but was told there was no call for such a school. He then tried the Manpower Services Commission (MSC) who turned him down because he was not an employer and, under their rules, they could not do business with an individual. He shared his ideas with Harry Lindley at the Doncaster Bloodstock Sales, and the dream might well have died there if Harry had not been inspired by Gordon and resolved to take the idea further.

Harry's scheme

Born in Hemsworth in 1919 and living in Intake, adjacent to one of Britain's finest racecourses, Harry Lindley had been around racing all his life. At different times he had been a jockey then a trainer and, although he never reached great heights at either discipline, he had a thorough grounding in his craft and an enthusiasm and love of racing that permeated his every thought. He did, however, have his moments on the track. During the war, while serving in the Royal Army Veterinary Corps, he was posted to the Middle East where the army used both horses and mules for transport in difficult terrain. While he was there he took the opportunity to do some racing and ended up as the Champion Jockey of Palestine.

Harry took a job as a school caretaker at Kingfisher School in the Doncaster suburb of Wheatley, and around 1976 he started to help youngsters get jobs in racing. Entirely voluntarily and unofficially, he would spend two or three afternoons a week at the Doncaster Careers Office, where his son, Michael, worked, encouraging youngsters to look for jobs in racing. It is estimated that, through Harry, around a hundred youngsters were given the chance to ride horses and learn about stable etiquette. Using his contacts throughout the racing industry Harry then found positions for some fifty of these youngsters in stables across the country. Teenagers responded to his teaching and former students recall how highly they respected him and the knowledge that he passed on to

Harry Lindley's childhood was largely spent in Sussex and his apprenticeship was served at the Duke of Norfolk's Michaelgrove Stables at Arundel. He held a Flat Jockey's licence in 1946, and a trainer's licence from 1946-48 after which he went out to Rhodesia (now Zimbabwe). Harry had a successful riding career in Rhodesia and South Africa, riding mainly for Lord Kensington, and he also had a short period as a trainer over there before returning to Britain in 1957.

He came to Doncaster, his wife's hometown, and in the late Sixties he began to train horses again at Tilts Farm in Bentley and later at Sandal. Training horses, however, was a highly competitive business and so in 1973 he was forced to give up training because his operation was just not viable. He continued to keep in close touch with friends in the racing industry, even though he was "outside" racing, and he was regularly called on to help with tending sick horses. He had "a million potions and lotions to cure any equine illness" and most of the time he would not take any payment; knowing that the horses were receiving the right care and attention was much more important to him.

Harry with a local owner during World War 2, when he was the Champion Jockey of Palestine.

them. It seemed to Harry that there were many other young unemployed people, who had never had the chance to ride a horse, who might be able to find a place in the horseracing industry if they could attend courses at a properly organised training school.

Herbert "Harry" Lindley, short of stature, as befits a jockey, had a big heart and was a man of deep beliefs. He was a member of the Labour Party, secretary of the Intake Branch L.P., and a union steward involved in TGWU affairs in Doncaster. He was dismayed by the plight of the young people he met in those years, who seemed destined to go from school to the scrap-heap, as Britain experienced the return of large scale unemployment. While many major manufacturing industries were either collapsing or becoming severely reduced in size, there was one British industry, Horseracing, that clearly did have a future, and one that was particularly relevant to Doncaster. The problem in that industry was the shortage of youngsters who wanted to come forward and work in stables, and, in some cases, go on to become jockeys. The transformation of British agriculture, the natural recruiting area for the racing industry, had witnessed a vastly reduced workforce on the land during the Twentieth Century, and those remaining were more familiar with tractors than with horses. Harry's scheme was a perfect fit to meet these two situations.

Gordon Blackwell in 1980 with "Inishpour" one of three horses he taught to do the "hat trick". At a signal the horse would pinch his hat and hold it aloft with a satisfied grin.

Gordon began his working career with horses in 1946, when he became a stable lad in Malton with Val Moore, having cycled over from his hometown of Leeds to see if he could get a job. Such was his determination that when he suffered a puncture on the way, he stuffed the tyre with grass and continued the journey to Malton as best he could.

In 2003 he had a race at Doncaster Races named after him. The 2.55pm race on the 24th January was called the Gordon Blackwell "Lifetime in Racing" Steeple Chase.

It helped to solve the employment situation for a significant number of young people and, at the same time, maintain the viability of the racing industry in terms of human resources. It was clear to Harry that what was needed was a properly constituted, adequately financed, training school that could organise relevant courses for potential stable staff and apprentices, and offer some form of recognised qualification.

These were still the days when Local Authorities were seen, especially on the left, as the fount of all social and educational action, so Harry first of all went along to his local council, Doncaster MBC, to see if they could help. However, by the early Eighties under the new regime of Mrs Thatcher, who was determined to reduce local government expenditure, local councils like Doncaster were desperately trying to hang on to the fullest possible provision of their core activities. They felt they could not afford the luxury of running and financing a new and untried project like a racing training school. Like Gordon Blackwell, Harry next tried the Manpower Services Commission (MSC), a relatively new player on the political scene, whose headquarters were in South Yorkshire at Moorfoot in Sheffield. They were keen to find alternative solutions for the creation of employment opportunities, as Britain's great traditional industries appeared to be crashing down around them. Again, Harry, operating as an individual, was rejected, although later the MSC would become a key supporter of the project and help realise the dream. Harry, who was one of life's natural networkers, now talked to some of his union and political colleagues. Mike Burns, then a South Yorkshire County Councillor (recently at 90 years of age the new Mayor of Hatfield) was chairing a meeting of the joint trade union stewards in Doncaster when he was approached by Harry with his proposal. He directed him toward another County Councillor, Colin Wedd, who was not only the Chair of the Doncaster District Labour Party, but also the Secretary of the all-powerful, majority Labour Group at County Hall. Perhaps even more to the point, he was a horse rider, who even rode to hounds; not a common activity among the members of the ruling Group of the "Socialist Republic of South Yorkshire".

Colin Wedd suggested that Harry should get a supporting resolution from the members of the Intake Branch of the Labour Party for his project, and then write to the Leader of the County Council, Roy Thwaites, and see what luck he had at County Hall in Barnsley. Leaders of councils get fifty proposals for action a day, and many have to be squashed pretty firmly, but Harry's idea appealed to Roy Thwaites, and he passed it on into the system to see if the council officers thought the idea had legs. If Roy had slung Harry's letter into the waste paper bin instead, it is most unlikely that there would be a Northern Racing College today at Rossington Hall.

So in March 1982 the letter found its way to the County Council's Employment Promotion and Development Unit (EPDU) and onto the desk of one of its planning officers, Jim Gale. Jim, along with his colleagues, was desperately and innovatively trying to develop schemes that would reverse the decline of the county's economy (1982 was year when the Steel Industry was in the forefront of the battle; two years later it would be the coal mines that were under attack). Jim was singled out by his boss because it was known that his wife was a keen horse rider. From such an almost accidental beginning, Jim Gale's long involvement with the Northern Racing College began. All the County Council people who handled Harry Lindley's initial request, Roy Thwaites, Colin Wedd, Mike Burns and Jim Gale, would play an important role in the subsequent history of the Racing College. Indeed, Colin Wedd and Jim Gale subsequently became the key figures in the development of the project over the next twenty-five years, from the first SYCC committee minute in March 1982 to the thriving College of today: a College that was recently awarded the very highest "outstanding" inspection grades by the Adult Learning Inspectorate.

As for Harry, he literally got to live the dream. He was consulted at every turn as the idea developed in the period before the SYCC opened the school on 1st July 1984. He sat on the steering committee, begged and borrowed the horses, arranged for placements for the first pupils and was the man who organised the training for the first few intakes of students. Now in his middle sixties, he was too old to be an employee of the County Council, which had a strict rule that staff should retire when they reached the statutory retirement age, to enable jobs to be freed up for young people or those unemployed. So, he was taken on as a consultant and he couldn't have been happier doing a job he loved in a new project he had initiated. He moved his caravan into the courtyard of the stables and lived on site for the next year and a half.

For Harry the story does not have an unclouded happy ending. By September 1985, ill-health forced him to hand over many of his duties to his newly appointed assistant, Bryan Rayner, who had come on board in August of the previous year to support Harry with the training and to take charge of yard duties for the students. Increasingly, however, he had to take over the running of the equestrian training operation as Harry's health declined, and in September 1985 Harry told the committee that he would have to resign, though he stayed on site until the New Year.

Harry Lindley died in 1987 aged 68, much mourned by those who had worked with him and studied under him. He suffered a heart attack on the day of the St. Leger, having gone out to some stables at Edenthorpe to tend to a sick horse. For a man with such a love of horses and an ability to connect with even the most difficult, it was not an inappropriate way to end his life. Like all people with a clear and successful vision his legacy survives him, and that legacy is the Northern Racing College of today. He would have been absolutely delighted to see how it has progressed from its earliest days of operation, so that now, in 2007, it is handling the training of over 200 students every year and undertaking numerous specialist areas of equestrian training as well.

Before the Start

1982–1984

The Northern Racing College, therefore, owes its existence to the South Yorkshire County Council, who first welcomed Harry Lindley's idea, gave it support and substance, and then ran the school for almost two years, from July 1984 until the demise of the Metropolitan Counties on 31st March 1986. When Roy Thwaites, the Council Leader, gave the project his blessing in early 1982, the South Yorkshire County Council was in its pomp and genuinely famous throughout the British political scene, as the "Socialist Republic" that had challenged the Callaghan Labour Government, and latterly Mrs T's Conservative Government, over its cheap fares transport policy. However, by the Eighties it had added another priority to its political programme and that was the creation of new jobs in an attempt to combat the worst unemployment that Britain, and especially South Yorkshire, had seen for four decades.

On 30th March 1982, the Employment Sub-Committee, a sub-committee of the Policy Committee, SYCC's "Cabinet", received Harry Lindley's letter about a racing training school and, after some brief discussion, resolved; *"that his letter be noted, and the County Council continue to provide advice and assistance if requested."* This rather anodyne wording was local government speak that could have meant that the project was being booted into touch, or, alternatively, that officers were quietly being instructed to give it life if possible. In the case of the training school it was the latter and Jim Gale was given the brief and told to make it happen. Within the Employment Promotion and Development Unit this was just another idea that might provide sustainable employment for a significant number of young people, because the EPDU were constantly, even desperately, exploring a disparate programme of numerous initiatives. These ranged from setting up speculative factory units and industrial estates for small businesses, youth training schemes in partnership with MSC, conferences and seminars, representation at major foreign and national exhibitions, local computer literacy courses, and innumerable requests for financial backing from local enterprises that were hoping to succeed in some niche market in the changing economy of Britain and the world.

Faced with a blank piece of paper, Jim Gale felt he must tap into Harry Lindley's expertise and ideas at the earliest opportunity. They agreed to meet at Doncaster Racecourse, which apart from being the home, since 1776, of the oldest classic race in the world, was also the venue for an annual show organised by the SYCC's Recreation and Culture Department, called the "Pageant of the Horse". For many SYCC councillors, most of whom represented urban wards, this show was their first and only experience of being in close proximity to horses. The "Pageant", which had been an overwhelming, if unexpected, success when it was first launched in 1975, may have been one of the factors why the County Council felt comfortable with Harry Lindley's proposal.

That afternoon at the races was an eye-opener for Jim Gale. While his wife, Sue, was a keen horse-rider, Harry Lindley's knowledge of all things equine was on an altogether different level. In the first five races, Harry amazed Jim by picking out the first and second placed horse in every race. Jim recalls how neither of them made a penny over this success, Harry because he did not gamble and Jim because he was too absorbed in the discussions to remember to go and lay a bet.

Finding A Home

The whole project of course would have been a non-starter if it had not been possible to find suitable premises. There was no way the County Council could afford to build new purpose-built facilities. So it was imperative that a stable block in reasonable condition could be found that was geographically convenient, of adequate size, and with enough land available for training. Fortunately, South Yorkshire, alone of the Metropolitan Counties, was not a conurbation and the majority of the land in the County was agricultural land, with its fair share of great country houses. Many of them had already been acquired and adapted by their local council for education purposes. A number came immediately to mind: Wentworth Woodhouse, situated near the point where Rotherham, Barnsley and Sheffield meet, is one of Britain's great secrets. Possessing the longest, and some would argue, the finest Palladian frontage in England, it had been considered, in 1973, as a possible County Hall for the newly established County Council. It had a magnificent stable block that would have graced a royal palace, but when Colin Wedd went along to look it over with Jim Gale, they soon realised that it would require too much investment to make it fit for purpose as a training school.

Colin Wedd, County Councillor and Secretary of the SYCC Labour Group, had been tasked by the Leader of the Council with keeping a political eye on the progress of the scheme. His role was to make sure Jim Gale got the necessary support to give the training school priority within the Council's departments and to clear any external political bottlenecks. He had played his part in encouraging the members to investigate Harry Lindley's idea and he would use his own contacts in Doncaster to find a suitable stable block that could be a base for the training school. After rejecting High Melton, a former country house, now a higher education facility, he met the Leader of Doncaster Council, Martin Redmond (soon to become an MP for Doncaster North after the 1983 Election), on site at Rossington Hall. Harry Lindley had flagged up the possibility of Rossington, whose stables had last been used by the Royal Army Veterinary Corps during the war. The Hall itself had been taken back into Doncaster Council's ownership in 1948 (the land had

Born and educated in Cambridge, Colin Wedd moved to the North when he went to Durham University to read Modern Languages at St. Bede's College. He came to South Yorkshire when he took up a teaching post at Don Valley High School and taught there for twenty-five years. He was elected to the SYCC in 1981 for the Doncaster Rural No.3 Ward (Brodsworth, Hampole, Hooton Pagnell, Sprotborough), and was quickly promoted to Labour Group Secretary because he was already a leading figure in Doncaster politics, having been the Secretary and subsequently the Chair of the District Labour Party. After the abolition of the County Council he became a member of the Doncaster MB Council in 1992 and was the Leader of the Council from 1998-2001. He was the Chairman of Doncaster Racecourse from 1997-2003 and has been the Chair of the NRC since its inception.

Jim Gale, son of a Durham miner, had followed the classic route of bright working class children in the post war era. The 11+ into grammar school, then on to university and after graduating moving on to a professional job far away from their home town or village. After gaining his degree in Town and Regional Planning at Sheffield University Jim returned to the area after a brief period in Cheshire, and secured a post with Sheffield City Council (1971-73), before becoming part of the skeleton staff setting up the new South Yorkshire County Council based in Barnsley. Although he had little experience of horse riding, Jim was an accomplished footballer in his youth who played for Sunderland Boys and Durham County Juniors, and was approached by both Arsenal and Manchester United to turn professional. If he acquired the brief to investigate the training school proposal almost by accident, it was to be a critical event in his life and for the next two and half decades he would be crucially involved in the development of the Northern Racing College.

originally belonged to them since medieval times but had been sold in 1838) and had served as a Special School for residential and day pupils since 1953. Martin Redmond was keen to support the project, and believed his Council would at least make the stable block available, at virtually no cost, to the new training school. He was less certain whether they would come in as full partners with SYCC. Nevertheless, the training school had found a

After the original 18th Century house had been destroyed by fire, W.M. Teulon designed the present Rossington Hall in 1882. A large and imposing country house, it had 22 bedrooms and included a stable block that became the home of SYARTS (now the Northern Racing College) in 1984. The Hall presently serves as a special school run by Doncaster MBC.

potential home in the architecturally impressive buildings, constructed in the early 1880s, containing 15 stalls and their own blacksmith's shop. These stables, always known at the NRC as the "Victorian Stables", with their curved brick elevation and imposing gothic gateway, reminded one observer of a stable block you might find in central Europe, although they did contain an ugly, 1960s indoor swimming pool covering almost one quarter of the stable yard.

Finding the Money

On 1st March 1983, almost a year after the County Council had first received a formal report about the training school, the Employment Sub-Committee received a fuller paper detailing the options for future action. Its author was Jim Gale, and in this paper he laid out the elements of the scheme that would be needed to get the school up and running.

- *Refurbishment of the stable block at Rossington Hall and purchase of an additional four acres of land for "schooling" purposes.*

- *Provision to be made for classroom instruction, including toilets, washroom and eating.*

- *Capacity for 48 youngsters to be trained in any one year: 4 x thirteen-week periods; 12 trainees per period.*

- *Two instructors; six horses.*

- *Potential trainees to be selected for interview by the careers officers of the four South Yorkshire District Councils. If selected they would receive an allowance of £25 per week.*

- *If possible residential accommodation to be provided for instructors and trainees.*

It was estimated that annual running costs would be £55,000, which would include a capital element of £11,000 for the refurbishment of the stable block. It was expected that in subsequent years the revenue costs would be nearer to £40,000, of which SYCC would be asked to find half . The big disappointment at the time of the meeting was that SYCC

The Victorian Stables before refurbishment. There was clearly a lot of work for the County Council to do.

had not persuaded the MSC, with their massive resources for supporting training, to show any interest in the project. Therefore it was left to local government to shoulder the bill, or find other partners, such as the European Social Fund, who might make a contribution towards the running of the scheme.

The final recommendation agreed at that meeting committed the County Council to support the setting up of the training school at Rossington Hall, but only if Doncaster MBC would share the administration and the costs of running it. They also instructed the officers to try again to get support from the MSC, but if that was not forthcoming to proceed, providing Doncaster was also prepared to jointly manage and finance the project.

It was two cheers for the progress so far. SYCC had thrown its hat into the ring but there was no certainty that Doncaster would be so enthusiastic, beyond making the stable block available at a peppercorn rent. In August a formal application was made to the MSC for Management Agency Status for a number of County Council projects that included the racing training school. This new application was handled by Jack Dyson at the MSC's York Office (Doncaster came under their jurisdiction), and there were more hopeful signs that they would support the Rossington scheme, after Roy Thwaites, who was an MSC Commissioner, pressed them to give the training school project a good hard look and see if something could be done to help. After some further questions about extending the scheme so that the courses would last a full year not just 13 weeks, they accepted that it could be administered under their Youth Opportunities Programme (YOP), the route that was flavour of the month at that time. An MSC requirement was that any appropriate trade union should approve of the scheme. So, after due consideration, Joe Daniels, the full time secretary of the TGWU Doncaster Branch, sent the MSC a letter on 11th August confirming that; *"the TGWU would have no objection to this proposed scheme"*.

If there was encouraging news from the MSC, there was gloom from two other quarters. Doncaster MBC, in November 1983, finally decided that they did not want to be involved in running or financing the school. Despite this, they did agree that they would stand by their provisional agreement to give a license to SYCC, initially for three years, to lease the Rossington Hall stables and four acres of land adjoining for a nominal rent, provided that SYCC met the costs of refurbishing the stable block and the surrounding land. SYCC were approaching a dilemma. Funding the total cost without any partner was a big ask and the Council was now operating under a sentence of death after Mrs. Thatcher, on the back of the Falklands War victory, called an early election and won an increased majority. Her party's manifesto included a pledge to abolish Ken Livingstone's GLC, which had been needling her government with their theatrical political gestures for some considerable time. Even more depressing for the "Socialist Republic", for good measure she also threw into the sacrificial pot the six metropolitan counties, which just happened to be controlled by the Labour Party.

Although the SYCC fought a two and a half year campaign to get this policy reversed, everyone else knew that they had been mortally wounded and would be abolished on 31st March 1986. This could have spelt the death of the Rossington Hall project; with no confirmed decision yet from the MSC to give financial support, and no support from Doncaster MBC who had their own problems with rate capping and the government's inexorable financial squeeze. Furthermore, another County Council faced with abolition, knowing that they were a dying political institution, might have felt any future initiatives would more sensibly be put on hold, and left for successor bodies to run with if they wished.

Fortunately for the Training School at Rossington Hall that was not the way SYCC councillors thought. Defiance was their middle name, whether the government was Labour or Conservative, and Mrs. Thatcher's abolition decision virtually guaranteed that they would use up their remaining reserves on schemes that they felt were worthwhile. Rossington Hall was now one of those favoured projects, and they resolved to make sure it happened as soon as possible and get the training school up and running for a couple of years before they were closed down.

The capital costs, once suggested as a mere £10,000, had now soared to an estimated £44,200, of which £6,400 was for the maintenance of horses and purchase of saddles, desks, computers and other equipment. SYCC approved a capital estimate to carry out the repairs to the Victorian Stables and provide kitchens, toilets and classrooms as well. In the event only the six stables were refurbished before July 1984 and the classroom and offices were accommodated in a temporary mobile building that remained in front of the Victorian Stables main entrance for five years. Two chemical toilets round the back of the stable block had to suffice until proper toilets were completed in 1989.

Early in the New Year the news came through that the MSC had approved the training school for funding as part of a long list of projects that the SYCC had submitted as their Youth Training Scheme (YTS) programme. Now, Jack Dyson, the Training Officer at the MSC's York office, was prepared to recommend £30,000, which was equivalent to half the costs of running the school in its first year. Jack was invited to represent the MSC on the newly formed committee, which would oversee the running of the project. Called a Programme Review Team (PRT) in SYCC parlance, it was chaired by Colin Wedd, who was the link to the members of the Council, and the professional administration was undertaken on a part-time basis by Jim Gale, officially the Project Leader.

The PRT membership was carefully selected to bring in all the relevant partners, most of whom had been involved in the planning to some degree already, but now also included Lieut. Colonel Richard Mackaness, representing the National Trainers' Federation and Tommy Delaney, who sadly died the following year, who spoke for the Stable Lads' Association. The school had also secured £5,725 from the European Social Fund because at that time Britain was considered one of the failing countries in the EU, with more than its fair share of unemployment blackspots. The SYCC picked up the remainder of the costs, which in the first year of operation, 1984-85, was £22,800, and the South Yorkshire Apprentice Racing Training School (SYARTS) was ready to go.

The Programme Review Team 1984

County Coun. Colin Wedd	Chair, SYCC
Jim Gale	Project Leader, SYCC
Frank Dever	Manager, SYARTS
Harry Lindley	Consultant
Jack Dyson	MSC
Joe Daniels	TGWU Doncaster
Mrs R. Griffiths	Doncaster MBC Careers Service.
Lt. Col. Richard Mackaness	Chief. Exec., National Trainers Federation
Tommy Delaney	Stable Lads Association

Up and Running

SYARTS 1984–86

The rather long winded name chosen for the new training school was also something of a misnomer. Opened on 1st July 1984, the school was called the South Yorkshire Apprentice Racing Training School (SYARTS), which rather suggested training apprentice jockeys, when its main purpose was to train youngsters to be stable staff with the possibility that a few would go on to become jockeys in the future. As the new school was funded by the County Council under their legal powers, there was a requirement that all the trainees had to come from South Yorkshire, and there were eight of them on the very first course. Equally divided between boys and girls, they did 13 weeks at Rossington Hall before going out on work experience placements at training stables across the country. Eventually, at the end of the course, which had included a week at Rossington Hall half way through their placement and a final fortnight's classroom instruction, five of them were found permanent positions in racing stables. One dropped out through homesickness, for many of the trainees had never lived away from home before, and this would continue to be a problem for some time. After a year the school had run four courses totalling 46 trainees, and a steady stream of applicants were already signed up for the next three courses, indicating that SYARTS was on to a winner. There was a fair attrition rate as only three quarters of the 28 boys and 18 girls had completed the course, but most of those who did complete, then got jobs in the horseracing industry, which only had about 300 new vacancies a year.

When out on placement during the course, the trainees often found the work very hard with long and unsociable hours. Some even thought that they were being unreasonably exploited, but at least they were working with horses at stables in attractive places all over England, such as Malton and Middleham in Yorkshire, Andover and Newmarket, even if some of these places were short on teenage entertainment. Harry Lindley had arranged most of these placements through his contacts, and the school relied on him to make other racehorse trainers aware of Rossington Hall's existence and offer places to SYARTS trainees. The trainees came from all four of the South Yorkshire Boroughs, with the largest number, unsurprisingly, from Doncaster and nearly all of them from urban areas. After living all their young lives on housing estates or in old terraced streets, they welcomed the fresh air of Rossington Hall, just off the Great North Road, along a tree lined drive that could have been the entrance to a small French chateau. Not that the area round about was very peaceful in 1984, because mining villages like Rossington were in the front line during the Miners' Strike and Bawtry, a mile away to the south, was a big transit base for police contingents that came up to South Yorkshire from all over the country to take on the miners on the picket lines.

The gaps in the staff team were also being filled. With little demand for structure planning by an authority about to be abolished, Jim Gale, the Project Leader responsible for the overall progress of the School, was now spending more and more of his time at Rossington Hall. Frank Dever, a former National Hunt jockey and trainer was appointed in the summer of 1984 to be the Manager and run the training operations of the School. Brian Rayner had become the Supervisor of riding and stable management training, with Tessa Delacour appointed to assist with training as well as supervise the trainees' programme of Life and Social Skills, which now included an additional P.E. element. Harry Lindley who wasn't overly familiar with the rigid bureaucracy of coursework, continued doing what he did best, and did naturally: instructing young riders and introducing them to stables for their placements. June Anderson completed the team and did all the typing and basic administrative work, and this relatively small team (there are now 27 full time staff in 2007), plus a group of landladies in the Doncaster area who provided "digs" for the trainees, delivered the courses that would enable the trainees to undertake a career in the racing industry.

As for the courses themselves, it was a little bit "seat of the pants", as SYARTS had to improvise as it went along. There were no NVQs at that time, as the National Centre for Vocational Qualifications was only established in 1986. Fortunately Harry Lindley had copious notes on just about every aspect of racing training, from how to muck out to grooming and riding the horses. The course-work became more structured after an unexpected visit from Derek O'Sullivan, the Director of the Irish Racing Academy and Centre of Education (RACE) in Co. Kildare, who invited a small group from SYARTS to visit their Centre that had been established several years before. In an industry that had a particularly high profile in Ireland, RACE was better resourced and was much further down the road than SYARTS, with fully planned courses supported by extensive training manuals. This was of tremendous benefit to Rossington Hall, and when the delegation returned home they adopted the Irish manuals as their own working documents, and the courses benefited from being on a more professional footing. There would be no fully accredited British course and qualification until 1991, and it would be Jim Gale and SYARTS that took the lead in writing the training manuals, after the MSC had threatened to pull the plug on funding the School because they were concerned that there were no nationally recognised qualifications.

On 22nd March 1985 the School was officially opened by the Chairman of the County Council, Terry Concannon, who came from Rotherham and would soon become a Trustee of the School. Although the refurbishment work had not yet been completed, the School was well enough established to merit a formal opening. A County Council has a vast array of skilled professional staff; architects, valuers, finance, personnel and pay-roll staff,

Malcolm Bygrave, now in 2007 the Training Manager at the NRC, was a trainee on the second ever course run at Rossington Hall. That was in 1984 and his group of thirteen were all girls, except for Malcolm and one other boy. Most of the girls had riding experience, one even owning a polo pony, but Malcolm came from Askern and knew little about horses, and while he was on the thirteen-week course he lived at home and cycled in most days. When he went out on placement it was to Clive Brittain's yard at Newmarket and this led to him getting a full time appointment there when his one-year YTS course was completed. Later, Malcolm would work for Charlie Nelson at Lambourn and Peter Calver at Ripon among others, and he obtained a jockey's licence and rode in 75 races.

When he was a trainee in that first year, Malcolm was selected to be part of a film report that ITV's "Breakfast TV" programme was doing about the new Training School. He was expected to ride behind the interview group and give a little authenticity to the filming. Instead his horse, Mr. Frodo, was spooked by a sheep that poked his head through the fence and frightened him. So, instead of calmly walking past the cameras to demonstrate that all was order and efficiency at the school. Mr. Frodo cantered by in total panic with Malcolm hanging on for grim life.

Malcolm returned to Rossington Hall, as an instructor in 1995 and moved up to Chief Instructor in 2006. In June 2007 he was promoted again to the key post of Training Manager. Of those original thirteen trainees in 1984, only two eventually made a full time career in the horseracing industry.

solicitors and engineers and they were now put at the disposal of the Racing School. SYCC Training Officers gave support and one of them ran a computer literacy course for the trainees, built around a programme called "Horses" that he designed to solicit the interest of the trainees in what was still a very new, and little understood, skill.

SYCC architect Paul Brooke, who would later design the outstanding residential block opened in 2003, drew up plans for the conversion of the Victorian Stables to provide classrooms and a meeting room, along with detailed plans for the refurbishment of the tack room, toilets, mess-room and the stables on the ground floor. The refurbishment work was done in two phases over the next five years and, thanks to the work done by Doncaster Community Volunteer Service (CVS), one of the myriad of initiatives around at the time to get young people off the dole and into the world of work, the final cost was only a fraction of the estimates, despite having to find an extra £6000 to treat unexpected woodworm and dry rot that had been found in the building. The first phase, the stables, was completed within eight weeks and a much needed all-weather Manège (the 50 x 40 metres outdoor training arena), also designed by County Council architects, was ready for use by the end of the year as well. It was modelled on the South Yorkshire Police's horse training facility at Ring Farm, Cudworth, near Barnsley, and had a sophisticated chevron drainage system to ensure its all-weather surface kept dry. It was the School's first building priority after the stables had been refurbished, but the other main priority, an indoor riding school, had to wait a decade before the School could afford it.

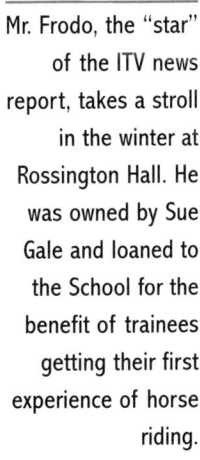

Mr. Frodo, the "star" of the ITV news report, takes a stroll in the winter at Rossington Hall. He was owned by Sue Gale and loaned to the School for the benefit of trainees getting their first experience of horse riding.

Riding for the Disabled

One of the first outside organisations to see the possibilities of the new facility at Rossington Hall was the Regional Committee of Riding for the Disabled (RDA) in South Yorkshire and Humberside. The RDA is a national charitable organisation working largely through volunteers, devoted to the provision of therapeutic riding for adults and children who suffer various forms of handicap. Association with horses has been found to have a very beneficial impact on individuals, and is also an excellent recreational activity for those who might otherwise lack the opportunity for exercise.

It was Alison Harris, then the Regional Chair of RDA, and now a Trustee of SYTT and Director of the NRC, who encouraged the founding of the new RDA group. She knew about Rossington Hall through her husband, John Harris, who was the SYCC Chief Executive and found the new facility ideal for the RDA's purposes. SYARTS were pleased to be asked to help and to demonstrate that other forms of equestrian activity could be undertaken on the site. SYARTS staff and students also gave valuable assistance as part of their work with horses at the School, and gained considerable satisfaction from their involvement, while Stancee Wedd has served as the Secretary of the Group from the outset.

In 2007 the Group now has five horses and runs five sessions a week for about sixty-five riders, supported by twenty volunteer helpers. Adult and child riders come from across Doncaster, from Conisborough in the west to Thorne in the east, and a group of volunteer fundraisers have to raise £500 each month to keep the group going. One of the stars of the RDA group at Rossington Hall is Sheila Bingham, who was the second Chair of the Group. An octogenarian and disabled herself; in 2004 she received an award recognising over a quarter of a century's service to the RDA. Sheila, who now lives in France with her daughter, has lived a very full life, bringing up a family and holding down a job, while she enjoyed horse riding and driving as her recreation. She was a founder member of the Rossington Hall RDA, as well as serving as the Chair of Brockholes RDA and was a most effective advocate for disabled issues

How to face the Future?

The incipient demise of the County Council spelt possible disaster for the Training School. Colin Wedd and the management team, as well as Council Leader, Roy Thwaites, had obviously been aware of the problem since the School had started, but it was now time in September 1985 to address the problem seriously and find a solution, otherwise the School would fold on 31st March 1986. Roy Thwaites raised the issue with his opposite number, Jim McFarlane, the new Leader of Doncaster MBC. The five councils (SYCC, Barnsley, Doncaster, Rotherham and Sheffield) had agreed a rough division of the

SYCC's facilities and assets along geographical lines where possible. So that Worsborough Mill and the Cooper Art Gallery would be run by Barnsley after 1st April 1986, Hatfield Marina (now Hatfield Water Park) would be taken over by Doncaster, while Rotherham would eventually run the huge Rother Valley Country Park on the boundaries of Sheffield and Rotherham. The logical solution for SYARTS was that it would be handed over to Doncaster MBC, as it was within their District and situated only three miles south of the town centre. Doncaster was reluctant to accept this, possibly for financial reasons, but, perhaps, because they would legally only have been able to pay for trainees from Doncaster and may have believed that they would not find enough recruits to fill the courses. Instead Jim Mcfarlane, shortly before his sad and early death in late 1985, made it clear to Roy Thwaites that he was prepared to support another solution that was being canvassed, namely that SYARTS become an independent charitable trust with Doncaster continuing to lease the buildings and land on very favourable terms.

The options for the School were limited. As it became clear that it was a non-starter to expect Doncaster to run the School alone, then perhaps the four District Councils together would run a joint enterprise as they would eventually do for the Police, Fire and Transport Services. SYCC was keen for such an arrangement to be set up, but this had no appeal to the District Councils. So the preferred, if only, option was for the School to become independent of local government, form a charitable trust, and chance its arm in the big bad world where you need to go out and raise your own finance. Such trusts have become commonplace in Tony Blair's Britain, but in 1986 it was a brave move to leave the financial shelter of a supportive Council and strike out on your own.

Roy Thwaites played a crucial role in starting and sustaining the development of SYARTS, later NRC. Born in Sheffield, he was an engineer in the steel industry, who was elected to Sheffield City Council in 1965. He became the Labour Group's Chief Whip and was also the Chairman of Transport. He opted for South Yorkshire County Council in 1973 because he was able to continue his work in developing the "cheap fares" transport policy. He was the Leader of the Council from 1979-86 and also held a number of national and regional positions, including Deputy Chairman of the Association of  Metropolitan Authorities and serving as a Commissioner for the Manpower Services Commission. He became the Deputy Chair of the Trust running the Training School at Rossington Hall in 1986 and held the post until 2004.

The new independent Trust's first priority was to ensure that the MSC remained as a long term funding partner. Then they needed to approach potential new partners, like the Jockey Club and the Horserace Betting Levy Board, with a view to getting financial support as soon as possible. Their only contact with the Levy Board before then had happened at the end of 1984, when, quite unexpectedly one day, an official at the Home Office had telephoned the School to enquire, on behalf of the Levy Board, who and what exactly was this new training school near Doncaster. Were they aware, he asked Jim Gale who took the call, that there already was a British Racing School (BRS), which had recently opened in its new premises in Newmarket in 1983. In fact, the SYCC did not know about the BRS when they set up the School at Rossington Hall, nor would it ever have occurred to them that they needed to ask anyone's permission to run a training school of their own. Nevertheless a meeting was fixed up in London to meet the Levy Board, but for reasons known only to them it was cancelled at very short notice, and there would be no help from the Levy Board until 1987.

By December 1985 a draft trust constitution had been approved and on 4th February 1986 SYCC, as a last gesture of support, agreed that all the assets and equipment on site, including saddles, tack and other equipment would be handed over free of any charge to the new Trust. Just as important, the Council also agreed a large donation of £100,000 to help the School through its immediate financial crisis, giving it much needed time to find new sources of income. These last minute bequests by the six Metropolitan Counties and the GLC were nicknamed "Tombstone Funding" and they all made some such payments. West Yorkshire Metropolitan County Council set up an arts funding organisation to survive after their abolition and the GLC gave many schemes in the Capital their support, although a considerable portion of their reserves must have been spent on a spectacular farewell firework party on the South Bank. There was an attempt by SYCC at the eleventh hour to add another £40,000 for capital projects, to the £100,000 already paid to the new Trust at Rossington Hall, but this was blocked by the Residuary Body that was winding up the affairs of the now defunct County Council.

The South Yorkshire Training Trust

The first meeting of the new Trust, to be known as the South Yorkshire Training Trust, was held on 21st March 1986, only ten days before the SYCC went out of business. The three Founder Trustees under the new constitution were Colin Wedd, who became the Chair, Roy Thwaites, who became the Deputy Chair, and Joe Daniels, who became the Honorary Secretary. Coun. Ron Gillies was nominated by Doncaster MBC to the place reserved for them and then Terry Concannon and Bob Johnston, the last SYCC County Treasurer and, briefly, their last Chief Executive, were co-opted onto the Trust, with Bob Johnston serving as Honorary Treasurer. After a certain amount of formal business, which included confirming all the existing staff in their posts and appointing Jim Gale as the part time Director, the meeting broke up and the press came and took photographs of the

SYARTS used the familiar logo of the SYCC as its badge until 1985. The neat and ubiquitous design, which incorporated the white rose of Yorkshire with green leaves that spelt out the letters SY, was chosen after a public competition in 1973. It proved to be very adaptable and was used for road signs, council buildings and throughout the County Council's departments and is still used by South Yorkshire representative sports teams and organisations today.

After 1985, SYARTS used a logo designed by Steve Wilkins of the SYCC Planning Department featuring three horses. He had been inspired by a photograph of three horses in a U.S. racing magazine. After 1990, on a suggestion of Howard Wright's, the middle horse was deleted and the two horse logo served as the School's badge until 2002.

new Trust members, at this historic moment for the Racing Training School.

South Yorkshire County Council's part in the School's history formally ends here. However its spirit lives on at Rossington more than anywhere else in the County, even though there are many surviving projects in the four boroughs that are part of the legacy of the "Socialist Republic". The Apprentice Racing Training School, now the Northern Racing College, has a special connection to the old County Council and many of the leading figures in its development over the last twenty-one years still partly define themselves as SYCC people. The former members of the SYCC feel aggrieved that they and their achievements, some quite controversial, have been airbrushed from history, even though there still is a County of South Yorkshire with its own Lord Lieutenant, but without a county council. At the end of March 2007, the South Yorkshire County Council Association of former councillors and senior officers, who still meet regularly, met to have a lunch to mark the abolition of the SYCC, twenty-one years previously. Appropriately the lunch was held at the Northern Racing College in the new residential building, and they were all delighted by the progress the College had made since the SYCC had set up the Trust in 1986.

Changing Horses

SYARTS and ARTS 1986-90

A newly independent body like the South Yorkshire Training Trust (SYTT) will always risk falling into a number of potential black holes which might jeopardise, or even kill off, the whole enterprise. So it was for the SYTT, the new parent body running the training school, still called SYARTS at this time. The first hurdle was easily crossed when the Charity Commissioners recognised them as a charity in their first month, but their biggest concerns were finding replacement funding for the protection afforded by SYCC's financial support and maintaining the vital funding from the MSC. They still had no guarantee of a lease for the premises, and just existed on little more than goodwill from Doncaster MBC, with a promise that a long-term lease could be negotiated. Settled now at Rossington Hall, they would probably have found it financially impossible to relocate in their present uncertain state. On the positive side, the School knew it was capable of delivering training on well organised courses, that it could attract recruits from among the local young unemployed, and could find placements at trainers' yards for its trainees. There was strong and confident leadership that intended to succeed, having proved themselves over the previous two years, and the new Board already had many members who were well placed to make friends and allies among the local establishment.

Finance was their first and major responsibility, as it is for most trustees or directors. Their ability to close the financial gap (running at a deficit of £11,000 in 1986 on their annual trading and rising to £22,000 in 1987) would ensure the School's survival. They would then be able to start the second phase of the refurbishment of the stables, establish a gallop and in the longer term build an indoor riding school and a residential block. For the moment, the lifesaving liquid asset of £100,000, received from South Yorkshire County Council before abolition, meant that they were in the black at the bank – indeed through prudent financial management, the Trust has never been overdrawn at the bank throughout its history – but that money could not support a trading deficit indefinitely.

The most alarming new situation in 1986 was that the MSC now insisted that SYARTS had to be an Approved Training Organisation (ATO), with properly constituted courses that met their criteria. Previously SYCC had been the managing agency and the MSC had dealt with them, but now the Trust was on its own and it had to satisfy the MSC all over again. If they failed to do so, there would be no MSC money and the School would have to close. They had till April 1987 to meet the criteria, although the MSC was prepared to continue funding for the moment providing the School changed to a two year YTS scheme, which, of course, doubled the amount of time that the trainees were with

SYARTS, and therefore added to the costs. In May 1987 the School only gained provisional ATO status, but this sufficed to safeguard the funding, although the MSC still queried their monitoring and assessment systems, even though seven out of their nine criteria had been satisfactorily met. Having cleared this major hurdle the School has continued to receive government funding ever since, even though the distributing agency has gone through many changes of name and form, later becoming the Training and Enterprise Council (TEC); it now manifests itself as the Learning and Skills Council (LSC).

We need Friends!

The new Trust needed friends, preferably with money and soon. The three obvious partners were, firstly, the four local authorities in South Yorkshire who had taken over most of the functions, responsibilities and premises of SYCC, and they made sympathetic noises. Secondly, there was the Residuary Body, the short life Quango that had been set up in 1986 to close down the business of the County Council and tie up all the loose ends. One of those loose ends was a second grant, this time for £40,000, approved in the dying days of the SYCC for the completion of the refurbishment of the Victorian Stables, but not paid over in time. This now lay with the Residuary Body who saw no reason why they should honour this "commitment" and, indeed, refused to do so. The Trust would challenge this position for the next three years but they would not succeed, and the money died with the Residuary Body. As it was a substantial sum it was worth chasing, and every person who might have influence, from Roy Thwaites to Sir Jack Layden (Leader of Rotherham MBC) and the Earl of Scarbrough, at one time or another tried to persuade the Chairman of the Residuary Body, Bernard Cotton, a leading Sheffield Industrialist, to release the grant, but he would not budge. The Residuary Body even taunted the Trust by telling them to seek counsel's advice if they did not like their decision, something that they must have known was too much of a financial risk for them.

The third potential partner was the Horserace Betting Levy Board that had been established after 1961 – when high street betting shops became legal – to ensure that some of the profits from betting on horse racing went back into the industry. There had been virtually no contact with the Levy Board before 1986 because SYCC did not need their financial help, but the situation had now changed. The Levy Board, and those who ran it, appeared to be part of the racing establishment and like others at Newmarket and at the Jockey Club were somewhat wary of this newcomer from Doncaster. The first appeal for financial support in 1986 was turned down flat and not unnaturally the Trust felt that they were being snubbed for all the usual reasons. Northerners have it hard-wired into them that the southern establishment never takes much notice of them, underrates their importance and is at best condescending. Such attitudes do have a precedent in rugby football. For a hundred years Twickenham declared it "illegal" for anyone to play their Union game if they had ever played, or even advocated, Rugby League. On the other hand, it may well have been that anything named South Yorkshire, whose County Council had delighted in calling themselves the "Socialist Republic" and where Arthur Scargill had his NUM headquarters, seemed, in the middle Eighties, about as acceptable as North Korea, to a sport with more than its fair share of aristocrats and millionaires.

What a spot of Royalty can do!

The Trust knew it had to change perceptions of itself within the racing world. Even though Yorkshire has nine racecourses, far more than any other county, and the first ever classic race was run at Doncaster in 1776, the racing industry regarded the British Racing School, recently relocated to Newmarket from Goodwood in 1983, as "the" training school: at the same time it regarded Rossington Hall, at best, as a place where you could do YTS courses and take up a job in the yards. Newmarket trained Jockeys, they were the "pilots", while SYARTS was seen as providing the "erks" of the ground staff. So it was important when Chris Howitt, from Rotherham, became the first SYARTS trainee to get

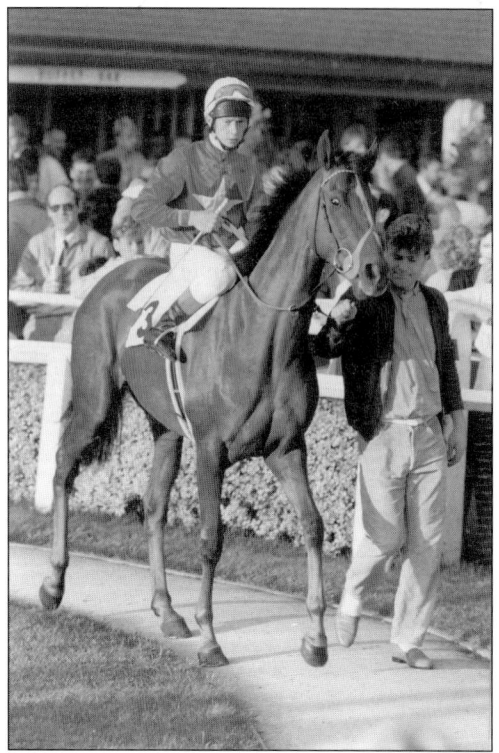

An important moment in the history of the School, when Chris Howitt of Rotherham became the first trainee to get a ride in public. He is pictured in the parade ring before going out onto the course at Catterick Racecourse in August 1986.

a ride in public at Catterick in August 1986, and other trainees got ten rides the following year, including the first apprentice to get a place, when Darren Stather, from Barnsley, came second at Chepstow in August. Two years later he would ride the School's first winner in a race at Bath.

There was one person who became a steadfast friend of the school after he had been approached to use his good offices to persuade Princess Anne to visit the School and consider taking up the Presidency of SYARTS. Richard Lumley, the 12th Earl of Scarbrough, was one of those chaps who really could walk with kings as well as commoners. He had long accepted that the political establishment in his patch – he lived at Sandbeck Hall, near Maltby, only eight miles from Rossington Hall – was for the foreseeable future going to be Labour, and working class Labour to boot, and he was very successful in gaining their acceptance. Unfailingly, he responded to requests from institutions in the county

The Earl of Scarbrough (left) with the Mayor of Doncaster, Coun. Ron Gillies, and Frank Dever (right) at the opening of the gallop in 1989

Richard Lumley, the 12th Earl of Scarbrough, was the President of the NRC for eighteen years. Educated at Eton and Magdalen College, Oxford, he served in a cavalry regiment, the 11th Hussars, in the Fifties and was ADC to the Governor of Cyprus in 1956. Later he was the Hon. Colonel of the 1st. Bn. The Yorkshire Volunteers from 1975-88. He owned racehorses, was a member of the Jockey Club and a Steward of Doncaster Racecourse. In 1996 he became the Lord Lieutenant of South Yorkshire, retiring in 2003 just before his death at the age of 71 in 2004.

to become their Patron or President, and having done so did his best to be useful to them when he could, and not just remain an aristocratic cypher. He contacted Princess Anne and she agreed to visit the School in June 1987, emphasizing that she did not want to spend the afternoon shaking hands with all and sundry, but instead to have a genuine fact-finding business visit.

The visit of the Princess went well, and like many other visitors she seemed impressed by the work being done and especially by the spirit and confidence of the staff and trainees. Subsequently, she did decline to be the School's President, but the visit had done the trick. Doors now opened, whether coincidentally or not, and the School felt it was getting more attention and respect, and some of that respect, it appeared, could be turned into financial help. The most important contribution came from the Levy Board, who made £12,000 available that year to aid the School's revenue spending, after Sir Ian Trethowan, their Chairman and sometime Director-General of the BBC, had visited the School while he was at Doncaster for the October Race Meeting. The Levy Board found an additional £9,000 the following year in 1988, and then began to support the School with very substantial capital sums that enabled the next phase of the development to take place, and the gallop to be constructed in 1988-89. They have remained staunch supporters of the School ever since. As for the Earl of Scarbrough, he now willingly accepted the Presidency in September 1987, asking only that the School spell his name correctly. He pointed out in a letter to the Chair, "That owing to the inability of a clerk to spell in1690, Scarbrough is not spelt like the seaside resort." He remained the President of the School until his death in 2004.

On the day of Princess Anne's visit the Derby was being run two hundred miles to the south, at Epsom. So, she joined trainees in the portakabin to watch the race on TV. As they watched she provided a commentary on the race, using her own experience of racing at the Epsom course.

Earlier she had been advised, by Colin Wedd, not to go into one of the boxes because the horse that was stabled there was rather unpredictable. To someone who had competed in the 1976 Olympics for Great Britain, this seemed a challenge rather than a warning. Ignoring the advice, she went straight up to the horse and patted it while the horse remained totally calm, if unimpressed with the rank of the visitor.

Elizabeth Gale, daughter of the School's Director, presents a bouquet on the occasion of Princess Anne's first visit to the School in June 1987

Three quarters of the cake!

Three of the local District Councils, Barnsley, Rotherham and Doncaster, now finally agreed a funding formula – based on the number of trainees who came from their District and were currently on courses – and backdated the money to April 1986. Altogether it came to £11,376 and if Sheffield City Council had paid their allocation of £4455, then the monies from the four councils would not have been too far off the amount SYCC had been paying annually to meet the School's deficit. Sheffield City Council was a different sort of political animal from the other three boroughs. Led by David Blunkett until 1987, it adopted some very public left wing positions – including prohibition of military displays and recruitment on its land and premises – and tended to be myopic about any project outside its boundaries. Whether it was because Doncaster MBC would not support the Crucible Theatre, Sheffield never made any grant to SYARTS, unlike the other three councils who continued to fund the School into the 21st Century. The Trust tried to interest other local councils in making donations after the recruitment of trainees was widened, and the name South Yorkshire was dropped from the title, but they were unsuccessful.

There was financial support from unexpected quarters. The Transport and General Workers Union, who represented the workforce in the racing industry made a covenant of £500 for three years, after their General Secretary, Ron Todd, a former Royal Marine Commando, and more to the point, an MSC Commissioner, visited the School and indicated that he wanted to help. A general fundraising letter soliciting support brought a £1000 donation from the Charitable Fund of Bass Brewery, although the Country Landowners Association and BBC Children in Need turned the School down. Coral UK, the bookmakers, agreed to sponsor the School's Apprentice Race that was first run at Doncaster on 26th June 1987 and has become a regular fixture. The race had two purposes. Firstly, to give SYARTS apprentices an opportunity to get a ride in public, whilst publicising the School's existence and encouraging trainers to give apprentices a placement at their yards.

The view from the Stables

Frank Dever, the Manager in charge of training, reported to each monthly Board Meeting. All his staff had been confirmed in their posts by the new Trust and they continued with their training courses as before, except they now had to cope with the demands of the two-year YTS courses. At an early stage Frank Dever suggested that it would aid recruitment and enable closer instruction to be given, if there could be more frequent courses with fewer trainees. So instead of 16 at a time every 12 weeks, the School now ran courses with 8 trainees every 6 weeks and it was also realised that the training would have to become more flexible, with specialised courses to cater for trainees with race-riding potential, as well as for those who wanted stud work and those who wanted to be stable lads and lasses (a phrase the School later dropped in favour of the less condescending, stable staff).

Frank Dever, pictured above on the extreme right, was the Training Manager at SYARTS from 1984 until 1993. The occasion is the presentation by the MSC of a plaque to mark the School's award as an Approved Training Organisation. Colin Wedd, the Chairman, is on the left.

Trainees on the two-year YTS course got an allowance of £27.30 per week in their first year and £35.00 in their second year, with a £40 lodging allowance and this would remain unchanged for five years. Not a king's ransom, but better than the dole and there was every chance of a job at the end of the day. Nevertheless, as the economy picked up and as the falling rolls in school in the second half of the Eighties reduced the number of school leavers, there were some concerns about recruitment for the first time. It was no longer sensible, or legally necessary, to restrict recruitment to South Yorkshire, and so a handful of places in 1986 were reserved for trainees from outside the county, with some coming from trainers' yards. By 1988, 30% came from outside the county, with Cheshire, Merseyside, Notts, West Yorkshire and Humberside providing the largest numbers, but with virtually every English county represented, even as far away as Cornwall. There was still a considerable attrition rate, but the great majority finished their course and the successful outcomes were well above the YTS national average.

There were other limitations on the quality of the course work. This was caused by the lack of some key facilities, like a gallop, an indoor school and more stable space. All of these had long been priorities for expansion but it was now time to press on with two of them. A suitable site had been identified for the gallop, north of the stables, that would have provided a straight course, but a part of the land was not in the Doncaster MBC's ownership. So it had to be abandoned in favour of the 53 acre area that lay along the main drive, with its eastern boundary abutting the Great North Road. Its acquisition depended on the finalising of a lease with Doncaster MBC, a process that was grinding on slowly as legal matters do. As for the Victorian Stables, the school only had a third of the total available and entered into negotiations with Rossington Hall School and Doncaster MBC to release some more. They seemed willing to make another eight stables available -they used them for storage – providing SYARTS found them some storage space to compensate. The final agreement also awaited the signing of the lease, at which point the School got the extra stables except for the area that Rossington Hall School used as a pottery workshop. This gave them a total of fourteen loose boxes and these were desperately required. The School needed to add to its number of horses, so that it could achieve a good mix of horse sizes and temperaments to test and accommodate the range of trainees' abilities. Frank Dever also believed the school would get a boost of morale and publicity if it acquired a "Big Name" horse, and at the end of 1987 "Primula Boy", who had won the Ayr Gold Cup, joined the stables.

Start of the international dimension

One of the most practical supporters of the School continued to be the Racing Apprentice Centre of Education (RACE) near the Curragh, in Co. Kildare, who offered to take a number of Rossington trainees on the second year of their course and put them through an intensive four-week period of training. This Irish experience was only for the most advanced of SYARTS trainees and the first six were accommodated at the Centre. RACE itself did not have any horses but the trainees did their initial training at the Irish Army's

Primula Boy, the winner of the Ayr Gold Cup, when 13 years old.

stables at the Curragh. However, it was an expensive exercise, which the MSC refused to fund, on the not unreasonable grounds that this was not only something of a "luxury" extra to the agreed programme, but was also outside the UK and therefore outside their remit. The course cost the School £200 per week per trainee, but all six trainees were offered jobs in Ireland as a result. The School once again learned by the Irish experience, especially the need for trainees to be physically fit. To help with the cost, RACE dropped the fee to £140 p.w. per trainee and the School later sent over a second group because it judged the benefit was so considerable. Contact was also made a little later with one (there are five altogether) of the French racing schools at Gouvieux. One SYARTS trainee took part in a cross-country race in France and came third, and later trainees from the Gouvieux School of Equitation would come to Rossington and be supervised on placements in Northern yards. It was the start of a happy association with similar racing schools in other European countries, which would lead in 2000 to the formation of the European Association of Racing Schools (EARS).

Changes of name, status and personnel

To reflect the changed circumstances, the School dropped the county's name from its title in August 1988 and for the next two years it would be known just as the Apprentice Racing Training School (ARTS). At the same time, in June 1988, it finally became a company limited by guarantee, something that the lawyers had been working on since October 1986, when the Trustees, all of them highly responsible but unpaid, became convinced that they needed the personal security of a limited company to protect them against any financial problems that the future might throw at the School. The changeover was seamless, with Colin Wedd remaining as Chair and Jim Gale becoming the Company Secretary. The Trust retained its charitable status, but it all added to the growing significance of the School. To mark this new phase the Trustees formally adopted the old SYCC colours of Purple and Green as their colours and adopted a new logo for Trust purposes.

All of the members of the Board of Trustees were retained, with the articles stating that there must be a minimum of five and a maximum of fifteen Trustees, with two places reserved for the nominees of Doncaster MBC (Coun. Ron Gillies, Chair of the Doncaster Racecourse Committee) and the TGWU (Brian Cox). Within the next year there were some useful additions to the membership, as people were brought

The logo of the SYTT, the South Yorkshire Training Trust, set up to run the School, after the South Yorkshire County Council had been abolished in 1986.

on who had specific experience in different areas of racing, as well as several with considerable clout on the national racing scene. In 1989, Lieut. Colonel Richard Mackaness, the Chief Executive of the National Trainers Federation, joined the Board. He had been supportive of the School since SYCC days and had served on the original PRT that ran the School before 1986. He had helped to smooth concerns at the BRS that the new Doncaster School was complementary to their programme and not a competitor, and his presence on the Board helped to make ARTS more acceptable to the racing establishment. So too did the appointment in 1990 of Howard Wright, a Doncaster lad, but now the highly respected Associate Editor of the Racing Post, the industry's bible. Mick McCoy, who was a former SYCC Labour Councillor and a top level football referee, who also had a lifetime's interest in racing and knew his way around the local racing scene, joined in 1989. Finally, in December 1990, Steven Astaire, a stockbroker and an amateur jockey and a new member of the Board of the Racehorse Owners Association, became a Trustee. He also owned a number of horses that he named after characters in the Marx Brothers films.

Many directors and trustees of companies, in reality, play little meaningful part in initiating ideas or making the real decisions of their organisation; rather, they rely heavily on the Chair and the professional executives to run the show, only sparking into life when they perceive that something is going wrong. The SYTT Board was not one of these; it was a hands-on board that was now so well balanced that it could aid the School with top class advice in many areas, giving leverage when there were "political" bottlenecks to be overcome. Steven Astaire, for example, was instrumental, along with Graham Orange and Howard Wright, in setting up the NRC Annual Charity Race Night at Pontefract Racecourse in May 1990, a great fundraising venture that in the first year brought in £23,000 and has become a fixture in the School's calendar. Joe Daniels, with his long experience in the TGWU, had taken on the task of setting up the staff contracts and terms and conditions in 1986, while Roy Thwaites, who had played his part in getting his former peers, the Leaders of the three Borough Councils, to support the School, was chairing a Fund Raising sub-committee aimed at potential major financial donors. Peter Calver, a trainer at Ripon, had been invited on to the Board in 1986, precisely because he was a man of substance in the racing industry. He was in fact the Vice-Chairman of the National Trainers' Federation and, as well as raising the School's profile in the racing world, he was a vet who regularly checked the School's horses for heart condition and other ailments, free of charge.

There were also changes in the staff of the school at this time. Bryan Rayner who had come on board in the earliest days, originally to instruct in stable training, moved on in 1987 to take up a full time appointment with Luca Cumani at Newmarket. He had been unemployed himself when he joined SYARTS and so the school had helped him to get back into a full-time career in racing as well.

A view of Pontefract Racecourse where the School first ran a Charity Race Night in 1990. Steven Astaire was consulted about the running of such an occasion as he had experience of running a successful annual event at Sandown. He suggested holding the event at Pontefract after Doncaster Racecourse, which initially seemed the obvious place, had turned the School down. He thought that the attractive and smaller Pontefract course, where all activity appears to be centred around the weighing room and the parade ring, would make for a better event anyhow. Graham Orange concurred, and set up the meetings with Norman Gundill, the Managing Director and Clerk of the Course, to complete the arrangements. Later, the event was moved to an afternoon meeting and the Charity Race Day has become an important annual event in the School's calendar. The proceeds from the day have gone into the SYTT's Development Fund, a large proportion of which was spent on the Residential Block in 2003.

Tessa Delacour left around the same time and initially she went out to Australia before returning to Europe. She eventually went to Ireland where she helped set up a stable staff training course in Co. Sligo.

They were replaced by Gill Beck, who had been the Head Lass at Chris Bell's stables at Pontefract and she was at the School for four years. From 1988 she ran the second year course of the YTS, eventually becoming a freelance consultant working with Jim Gale's firm, Profile Planning Services and eventually taking up a post with the new RTBTB. Carol Bowman arrived in the Spring of 1987 as well. When appointed she was currently the Point to Point Trainer at Firbeck, and at Rossington Hall she worked in tandem with Gill Beck for a number of years, before leaving and serving as an External Verifier for the BHTB.

Lease, refurbishment and gallop

The Phase 2 refurbishment and the development of a gallop were dependent on getting the lease finalised. The Levy Board had indicated that they were willing to find substantial capital monies, but no one was going to spend money on buildings or projects that could be whisked away by the landowner. Eventually in December 1987 there was a firm proposal from Doncaster MBC that they would grant a 21 year lease for the stables, the surrounding land and the 53 acres field where a gallop could be built. The catch was that this would no longer be at a peppercorn rent, but would be charged at a full commercial rent that was judged to be £5873 in first instance. Doncaster may have felt that, as they were now making a grant to the School of a similar magnitude, they were therefore, in effect, giving a lease free of charge. Not a view shared by the School, but they agreed to the terms in February 1988 and subsequently in 1996 the lease would be extended to a 99-year lease. However, for the present the Trust had to wait over a year before the documents were finally signed and sealed in August 1989.

Despite this delay the Trust felt confident they could now complete the refurbishment of the eastern section of the second floor of the Victorian Stables to provide offices, a trustees' meeting room, mess room, tack room, kitchen, toilets and a linking staircase. The School could manage the costs because a large percentage of this work was carried out by Doncaster Community Voluntary Service (CVS) free of charge. Their contribution, which came from Government funding, was incalculable and it was a great loss when they went out of business in 1989. This phase of the refurbishment included pinning the attractive clock tower which was in an unstable condition, and, as an extra, the clock was mended and cleaned up for a cost of £122 after a long "coma" of inactivity

When the Tack Room was completed in 1988, the School decided that it would dedicate it to the memory of Harry Lindley, who had died the year before. After consultation with Joan, his widow, it was decided that it would be appropriate for a small plaque, commemorating Harry's part in the formation of the School, to be placed on the wall of the Tack Room and it is still there to this day.

Soon afterwards, another phase of the refurbishment of the upper floor of the Victorian Stables created a classroom and more offices, accessed by a new staircase at the west end of the yard. The Levy Board agreed £69,000 capital grant towards this stable block refurbishment and another £12,000 for furnishings and fittings. When it was all done the School could finally get rid of the old portacabin on the front lawn that had been their only mess, office and equipment facility for four years. The full grant from the Levy Board, including £51,000 for the Gallop (of which £20,000 was for compensation to the tenant farmer, plus fencing, surfacing and seeding), came to a grand total of £132,390 and this was substantial money. Their decision also served to convince the racing world that one of the establishment heavyweights was backing SYTT and its racing school.

Opening the Gallop

Lester Piggot had been invited to open the gallop but he could not make it. So on 16th May 1989 the honour fell to Martin Brennan, Liam O'Hara and National Hunt jockey, Mark Dwyer, who were accompanied on a ride round the six and a half furlong course by

The Friends of SYTT

To aid local fund-raising a "Friends" group had been suggested back in 1986 by Terry Concannon, but it was not until late 1988 that a meeting of interested supporters was called at Rossington Hall to establish the "Friends of SYTT". That inaugural meeting in November was full of enthusiasm and a date was fixed in the following January to form a committee and elect officers. On 19th January 1989, Michael Burns, a former SYCC Councillor and the man who had first steered Harry Lindley towards the County Council, became the Chair with Mick McCoy, another former SYCC Councillor, soon to become a Trustee, elected as Vice-Chair. The new committee pledged to raise enough funds annually, on behalf of the school, to bridge any deficit that occurred in the revenue budget. They were good to their word and over the last eighteen years they have raised over £100,000, most of it going into the general kitty, but some for specific projects such as the mini bus purchased in 1999 to bus trainees to and from Finningley, and also take them on outside visits.

Apart from soliciting individual donations, the Friends quickly produced an ambitious programme of fund-raising events. Their first event was a Wine and Cheese Buffet in August, followed by a formal Dinner in October at Doncaster Racecourse that raised £875. An Open Day in November attracted 500 people to a number of horse-centred activities at the School and helped to publicise the School's existence in the area through good press coverage and general goodwill. In March of 1990 the Friends held a "Race Night" at Hatfield Country Club, an occasion when people can forget that they are only looking at a screen and get quite carried away, shouting loud encouragement at the "horses" on which they have laid bets. By 1990 there were 63 members of the "Friends" including one or two institutions, like ASLEF, and also a little known MP, one Tony Blair. He had visited the Doncaster Races, and Mike Burns, in his characteristic way, had weedled a subscription out of him. He had no such luck with John Prescott, who visited the School about the same time, and who was photographed by a national newspaper riding the horse simulator. In September 1990 the Friends of SYTT adjusted their name when the School became known as "The Northern Racing School", so for a time they were called the "Friends of Northern Racing School" until another name re-alignment replaced the title School with College in 1995.

four ARTS trainees. They reported that the surface seemed excellent with none of the usual kickback experienced on gallops of this type. However, it would soon prove too hard a test for some of the School's elderly horses, causing some of them to go lame. One horse "Call me Morlais" had died as a result of a heart attack suffered on the gallop and others had leg problems, possibly because they had been retired from racing owing to leg injuries. Many of these horses were loaned and their owners would be unimpressed if harm came to them, so time on the gallop was rationed and it was only used twice a week to spare the school's horses. The whole area of the field where the gallop was situated was seeded with moor and heath grass rather than parkland and it could be cut for silage, or earn some money by letting sheep graze on it.

Gentlemen and Players

By the middle of 1990 the School was established in its own operations, accepted by most of the racing industry and was a leader in the new training courses and qualifications. It continued to find allies among leading figures in the racing world, after they were first persuaded to visit this northern upstart that they had barely heard of, and subsequently were amazed at what they saw on the ground at Rossington Hall. One key visitor, in September 1989, was the new Senior Steward of the Jockey Club, the Marquess of Hartington, later the 12th Duke of Devonshire and now the President of the Northern Racing College, who wrote to Colin Wedd after the visit saying;

> *"I have to say the afternoon was an eye-opener. I am a firm believer in the value of training for all involved in horse racing and of course SYTT is dealing with the most important section of the workforce, because they are the youngest and the future of the industry."*

Michael Burns was the first Chair of the Friends of Northern Racing College. A former Chairman of the County Council (he is seen here in his formal chain of office), he had been a tank commander in the Fife and Forfar Yeomanry during the Second World War. He was a veteran of the Normandy campaign and was part of the spearhead that re-captured Antwerp in early September 1944. He was an enthusiastic fundraiser for the Training School during the period he served as the Chair of the Friends from 1988 until 2004.

With support in such high quarters within the industry, the School could look all doubters squarely in the face. Training was one area where ARTS had the edge. Created by a county council that was modern and progressive in its administrative processes, and dedicated to tackling the employment problems created by the changing industrial world, they willingly adopted the new rubrics of training and qualification for young people. In the late Eighties, Britain was undergoing a huge social and economic sea change. Driven by Mrs. Thatcher's government, in many parts of the country this left numerous workers adrift on the beach, but also made the country face up to its poor economic performance compared to other nations in Western Europe, North America and the Far East. Unenthusiastic about comprehensive education, her party, and its industrial supporters, looked to systematic training and properly verified national qualifications as the way to build up a skilled workforce to restore Britain's economic condition by the end of the century. "Training, Training, Training" might have been their slogan; it definitely was their policy when they set up the National Council for Vocational Qualifications in 1986.

The racing industry, a bastion of tradition and the Establishment, may have been slow to realise that this would apply to them. After all there were yards that still operated schemes that were medieval in origin, where an apprentice was indentured with the parties to the contract named as master, apprentice and father, with the father having to pay over a surety to the master for the apprentice's good behaviour. However, there were enough people to see the light, and if some did not it was made clear that there would be no government funding unless they went along the route of nationally recognised courses and qualifications. In 1987 the Joint National Horse Education and Training Council (JNHETC) was established with Christopher "Kit" Barclay as the chair, with membership from almost every acronym in the industry, including the BHS, BSJA, TBA, ABRS, BRS, etc. and ARTS, with Jim Gale becoming a member of their council.

Yet, while other sections of the JNHETC were prepared to accept national qualifications, the racing industry was still dragging its feet. Jim Gale wrote a paper in late 1988 entitled "Future Training in the Horse Racing Industry" in which he stressed the need for embracing NVQs and advocated a training board should be established by the industry to run these qualifications. The upshot was that the JNHETC set up a Racing Training Working Party in April 1989, which included the NTF, the Jockey Club, the Levy Board, and the Racehorse Owners Association, with Jim Gale and Gill Beck playing a leading role in its deliberations. From this group came a decision to form the Racing and Thoroughbred Breeding Training Board (RTBTB), whose first task was to draw up and pilot a Level 1 NVQ for the racing industry. Jim Gale became the Manager of the RTBTB and its administration and the Candidate Registration Centre were based at Rossington Hall. The pilot was ready by March 1991, but ARTS had already been using it earlier and ironing out its bumps and sharp corners. The School, and especially its Director, was becoming the midwife for the delivery of training qualifications for the whole industry and the status of the School was rising accordingly.

The Consultant

Jim Gale's official profession was a town planner, and for the next thirteen years he acted as a consultant planning inspector for the Planning Inspectorate. As the SYCC was dying in 1986 he left local government and set himself up as a consultant, something that was very fashionable at the time. While many so-called consultants never found clients willing to consult them, Jim prospered and over the years he has written more than 1400 planning decision letters as a planning inspector. He set up his own consultancy firm, Profile Planning Services, and acted as the Director of the School on a consultancy basis for three days a week until 1997 when he became the full-time Director. He was the Manager of RTBTB and Secretary of the JNHETC on the same basis, while at the same time he continued with his work as a planner, including serving private clients.

Another name change

At the April Board Meeting in 1990, just four years after the School had been cut adrift from SYCC, Colin Wedd proposed that the school's name should now become "The Northern Racing School". This was felt to have more gravitas than Apprentice Racing Training School, and producing apprentice jockeys was, in fact, only a small part of its work. The inference was that Rossington Hall would largely serve the North of England, and perhaps Scotland, and the BRS at Newmarket, although in East Anglia, would serve the South. It was a confident Board that could look back on how far it had travelled in those four years. Regularly there were around 90 trainees on courses at any one time, there were 19 horses in the stables and 29 former trainees had had rides in public. In June 1990 Claire Balding, whose father was a trainer at Bawtry, became the School's first female trainee to ride a winner when she won at Edinburgh. Then in April 1990 at Sandown Racecourse, a "summit" conference was held for the whole of the racing industry. Everyone who was anyone in the racing world was there, and the welcoming address was given by Lord Hartington as Senior Steward of the Jockey Club. Colin Wedd and Jim Gale were among the invitees and Brian Cox, on behalf of the TGWU, was one of the speakers. One of the main thrusts of the conference was the importance of properly administered training in the industry. The Northern Racing School was now on the inside of the rails, if not yet part of the Establishment.

A Bumpy Ride

NRS 1991-1995

If, by the start of the new decade, the NRS seemed well established, the next few years would demonstrate that the School might still be vulnerable to outside forces that could seriously effect its future progress, even its survival. There would be a long saga about signing a 99-year lease with Doncaster MBC; the ambitious plans for new facilities at Rossington Hall would take several years to realise, and the much needed residential accommodation on a site adjacent to the stables was still on the drawing board when the century came to an end in December 1999. The racing industry, led by the Jockey Club, instituted a thorough-going inquiry into training that resulted in the Struthers' Report of 1992, followed, in 1993, by the RTBTB sending an international firm of accountants to make a financial and administrative appraisal of the NRS and the BRS. Both initiatives could have adversely affected the revenue support from the racing industry, where many still asked the question, *"do we really need two racing schools?"*

Meanwhile, if you were a trainee everything at Rossington Hall would appear to be running very smoothly. Frank Dever remained the Training Manager until ill health forced him to retire in 1993 when Mark Beecroft took over, and after 1991 there was a clear path of NVQ courses that would lead first to Level I and then to Level II. In the summer of 1991 seven trainees achieved Level II NVQ's, the first in the country, and outstanding students could then go on to attempt Level III, which was introduced in 1993. Again the first successful candidates to pass Level III in the whole of the country were from the NRS, but this initial group were all staff members, including Mark Beecroft and Kevin Frost, as well as Martin Bielby who left shortly afterwards after six years at the NRS, though he was still in contact with the School in his new role as an Internal Verifier. Trainee allowances were also raised in 1991, so that now a trainee over seventeen years of age could get £45 per week, a rise of £10. The number of trainees remained around the 80 mark during the first few years of the decade, but in 1994, for the first time, the century barrier was crossed when 108 trainees were recorded on the school's books. The gender balance of the students in that year was close to equal, with 52% male and 48% female, a point of some satisfaction to the School.

In April 1991 at Fakenham, Duncan Clooney became the first NRS trainee to ride a National Hunt winner, and in the summer, Jane Hindmarsh rode the School's first Point to Point winner. By November 1992, the School could boast 353 rides in public, including 28 winners, of which Tony Garth had ridden 13, and many of these rides were in the Apprentice Racing Series, where NRS trainees competed with riders from the BRS. The

Frankie Dettori visited the School in 1991 and took a ride around the gallop, followed by one of the NRS's trainees.

series was held at seven different racecourses, with the NRS responsible for organising three of these races, at Doncaster, York and Redcar. The School was keen that the series would adopt a "no whip" policy because they believed it was better for the horse, especially if apprentices got carried away, whilst trainers and owners would be happier to lend their horses for apprentice races if they felt their welfare was not compromised. However, the Jockey Club, who refused to ban the whip, overruled the NRS. There were other sporting successes for NRS trainees, when four of them became national champions at their weight in the Stable Lads' Amateur Boxing Association's Tournament, a black tie occasion held at the Hilton Hotel in London.

Struthers Report 1992

In 1991, the Stewards of the Jockey Club, concerned that no-one had a handle on the training requirements of the racing industry, or how they could be funded in a sustained and equitable way, asked their Deputy Senior Steward, Andrew (Sandy) Struthers, a Glasgow shipping magnate, to chair a working party to undertake a comprehensive review of the whole issue of training within the industry. The NRS was delighted to take part in this group, that had representatives from eight bodies (all the usual suspects, including the Racehorse Owners Association, Jockeys' Association of G.B. and the Thoroughbred Breeders' Association) plus the BRS and the NRS, who were represented by Colin Wedd and Jim Gale.

The NRS wanted two specific decisions from the Working Party, apart from a general willingness to support a systematic NVQ based training regime throughout the industry.

Firstly, they wanted the Struthers Report to clearly accept the continued existence and future important role of the NRS within the racing industry. No group had formally questioned the NRS's right to exist, but in that very English way when men of influence meet, it seemed to the NRS that there was always more than a whiff of disapproval aimed at "that school at Doncaster", which had never sought their "permission" to exist and which they themselves would never have set up in possible competition to the BRS at Newmarket.

The second major concern for the NRS, and it was almost a litmus test of their acceptance, was the distribution of monies under Rule 194 of the Rules of Racing. This rule said that a small portion of the £50 million prize money won in races at British courses should go to training. Since 1983, this Rule 194 money had been one of the main funding streams that financed the BRS, and even if it was a very small percentage of the prize money it produced over £250,000 per annum. It was Steven Astaire's suggestion that the NRS should request that some of this largesse, on a pro rata basis, should be shared with them. The NRS argued that they also were serving the training needs of the industry, and despite considerable YT funds from the Government via the TEC (something the BRS in Suffolk had only just begun to consider applying for), they were always short of revenue funding.

In its findings the Struthers Report supported the NRS on both counts. Throughout the recommendations the assumptions were that both schools would deliver the training needs of the industry. Recommendations 5 and 6 read:

"That the considerable investment already made in the two schools should be utilised to the full by expanding their facilities to train up to 300 recruits each year (180 BRS and 120 NRS)."

"That the BRS and the NRS be asked to establish training courses for NVQ Levels II to IV as soon as possible, and other training courses for the industry in the future as requested by the RTBTB"

The NRS's legitimacy was therefore established, and on the issue of Rule 194 it was proposed, and subsequently accepted, that the money should go into a general pot, along with Levy Board contributions, and then be apportioned by the RTBTB after an annual review of each school's programme. The RTBTB was to be strengthened and charged with being the body with responsibility for *"a comprehensive training policy and qualification structure throughout the industry"*, based on NVQ's up to Level IV. Nine of the organisations on the working party, including the NRS, plus the BHB and the National Stud, became members of a reconstituted and strengthened RTBTB Board, with Sandy Struthers continuing as the Chairman. Jim Gale's consultancy, Profile Planning Services, who had been running the RTBTB for three years was now pushed aside; perhaps because he was not considered neutral enough to run the new funding regime, and Richard

Mackaness was appointed to the new key post of the Executive Training Officer, with Gill Beck as his senior assistant.

Never believe accountants!

Given its increased status, the new RTBTB started to flex its muscles and appointed a well-known, prestigious firm of accountants to undertake a management and financial review of the two racing schools. The report was ready by December 1993 and it had the SYTT Board spitting blood. Firstly, they were appalled that they had not been able to comment on an interim draft, when they could have corrected all of the many inaccuracies, and therefore they felt the report carried assumptions that misrepresented their management and financial practices. It was perceived by the SYTT Board as too favourable to the BRS, and they were particularly annoyed that the report repeated the old stereotype, that the NRS was essentially a vehicle for YT youngsters to lift them off the dole, while only the BRS aimed at producing recruits for the racing industry of the highest quality, ruthlessly "weeding out" youngsters who were deemed to be not good enough.

The report's main concern was that the BRS, with 12 full and part time staff and 52 horses, processed 200 students each year on a budget of £654,000 p.a., whereas the NRS with 10 staff plus a consultant director and 23 horses, had only 80 trainees a year and had a budget of £593,000 p.a. (The NRS's income included £479,000 from the Government via the TEC, £42,000 from the Levy Board and £75,000 which they raised themselves from other sources). On the face of it the authors of the report had a point, but, more controversially, they also stressed the potential – though not actual – difficulties of the Director's post being held by a consultant who officially only worked for the NRS for four days of the week, and recommended a full time Manager instead.

As if in sympathy with the Board's anger, two of the School's horses indulge in a little rumbustious action of the own at Rossington Hall.

The SYTT Board fired off their reply to Sandy Struthers, the Chairman of the RTBTB, stressing how the two day visit had hardly afforded sufficient time to produce anything but a snapshot of NRS working practices, and furthermore had not compared like with like over the finances of the two schools. It was pointed out that the NRS ran twelve-week initial courses whereas at the BRS they ran for only nine weeks, and only the NRS had to pay for trainees' lodgings and allowances, which made a huge difference to the NRS's expenditure. There were also additional staffing costs caused by the continual demands for information from the TEC. Some of the recommendations, in the time-honoured ways of consultants, were suggestions from the Trustees, Director and staff of the NRS that were being quoted back at them in the report.

To be fair to the accountants, they also queried the £175,000 cost of the administration of the RTBTB, which they felt took a rather large percentage (14%) out of the monies available for training by the schools. Many of their recommendations to both schools were concentrated on adopting the new fashionable management practices of non-financial performance targets (financial controls at both schools were regarded as good), feedback from trainees and trainers' yards, and benchmarking of educational and administrative practices with foreign racing schools and training in other industries in the UK.

Having got their anger off their chests, the School followed up some of the suggestions. All agreed that there was an imperative for the RTBTB to produce an overall strategy for training for the racing industry which the schools could follow, while the schools themselves needed to produce their own development and business plans. The next period of friction between the schools and the RTBTB came after Brigadier Richard Nash had replaced Lt. Colonel Richard Mackaness as Director of Training in 1995, and he appeared to want to expand the control of the RTBTB over the two schools. In the racing world, where military rank carried influence, Richard Nash was a senior appointment, but this cut no ice with the civilian meritocrats at Rossington Hall, who quickly made the point that he was not their line manager and that they were an independent trust which saw the RTBTB as an enabler, not as a body taking the executive lead. After a while Brigadier Nash moved on, but not before the NRS was put through another financial appraisal, this time by the Director of Finance of the BHB in September 1996.

Delays over the Building Programme

Comparisons with the BRS always reminded the NRS that they needed an Indoor Riding School and on-site residential accommodation, both of which existed at Newmarket. Both projects were expensive and although a development fund had been started in the Eighties with monies from the Pontefract Charity Race Night, it only stood at £58,000 in 1991. The Indoor Riding School was vital to allow training to continue during inclement weather and in the dark winter evenings, and it could also be hired out and be a revenue earner. The residential accommodation would obviously improve "esprit de corps" and a sense of belonging among trainees, but it was also an imperative because there was a shortage of suitable landladies, and they were inconveniently dispersed around the Doncaster area. In 1991, Paul Brooke, the former South Yorkshire County Council architect, was again asked to draw up preliminary designs and he planned for a building whose exterior elevations complemented the stable block and provided 30 bed spaces in double rooms. The original plans were costed at £1,500,000, and the school was not over-pleased that Sandy Struthers continually referred to it as "Caesar's Palace", indicating his belief that it was rather over-elaborate.

Part of the delay was caused by the protracted negotiations to sign a 99-year lease with Doncaster MBC. They seemed willing to offer such a long lease, but negotiations dragged on until February 1996 when it was finally signed. The presence of Rossington Hall Investments, a company chaired by Sir John Hall of the Metro Centre, Gateshead, and Newcastle United fame, also muddied the waters as he had bold schemes for the site. His plans included two golf courses, one of which would be to international tournament specifications, probably using Rossington Hall itself as a St. Andrews style clubhouse. Planning permission for both the Riding School and the Residential Block was sought at the end of 1992 but was not granted until much later. Meanwhile the Board of SYTT knew they had to raise more finance themselves, that would hopefully act to lever in substantial capital funds from the Levy Board. If they could be persuaded to grant aid £500,000, then it would, eventually be possible to realise the dream of better facilities at Rossington Hall. In the meantime a Fund Raising Sub-Committee, chaired by Brian Cox, was established in 1992 to tap into big sponsorship from successful large, local businesses, with a very ambitious target of £2 million for the Development Fund.

If the School had to wait for the major projects, there were other smaller items that could be paid for at an earlier date. In 1993 the School purchased a Racehorse Simulator for £9,000 for use with advanced trainees as well as early learners. Nine loose boxes were purchased as the School increased its number of horses (there were 28 by 1993) and £10,000 was provided from the Development Fund to enable more suitable horses to be bought. In November 1993 construction started on a new manège, a cross-country course was constructed a year later and in 1995, for a cost of £7513, the Grey Barn was converted to form a stable block, enabling 14 more loose boxes to be accommodated. A horsewalker was purchased in April 1994 with money that had been earmarked for refurbishing the Lodge at the bottom of the drive. The Board had been pursuing this facility since 1991 to enable a member of staff and their family to live on site in a proper home rather than a caravan, but it eventually became clear that refurbishment at a suitable cost was impossible, with the electrics alone costing £20-30,000.

One windfall the School did enjoy came from an unexpected source on the other side of the world. The Royal Hong Kong Jockey Club had made a substantial grant to the BRS and Howard Wright investigated to see if they were prepared to help NRS as well. It may

The new Library built with the generosity of the Hong Kong Jockey Club and situated on the upper floor of the Victoria Stables.

have been that they were uncertain about their future after 1997, when Hong Kong was due to be handed back to China, but they indicated in early 1995 that they were prepared to make a grant to the School of £15,000. Rather than put this into the general pot, the Board decided to use it to establish a Library in the Stable Block and name it after the RHK Jockey Club. To mark the gift one of the races at the Pontefract Charity Race Night was named after the RHK Jockey Club, and when the library was opened the School invited their Chief Executive, Major General Guy Walker, to the opening ceremony performed by the Mayor of Doncaster. He suggested that the title Royal might now be dropped, as it would appear more diplomatic when the colony reverted to control by the Peoples' Republic.

New People, New Logo, New Name

The core membership of the SYTT Board stayed pretty constant during the Nineties, but there were some comings and goings. Graham Orange, the PR Officer for the trailblazing marketing organisation called "Go Racing in Yorkshire", that serves the nine Yorkshire Racecourses, had already helped with setting up, and subsequently running, the Charity Race Night at Pontefract. He now joined the Board and brought racecourse experience to its deliberations, as well as some extra public recognition as someone involved in the televising of racing. In November 1991 Brian Cox ceased, on his retirement, to be the TGWU representative on the Board, but he stayed on as a Trustee and the Union after a period appointed Tim Lyle, their National Organiser. Mick McCoy's sad death in 1994 caused another vacancy, as did the departure of Bob Johnston, the Honorary Treasurer, who moved up to the Lake District. He had played a most useful role in guiding the Trust through the financial pitfalls of its first ten years and in recognition of his service to the School he was made a Vice President. This position had been created in 1991 to honour particular supporters of the NRS, and one of the first VPs was Sir Jack Layden, South Yorkshire's leading local government figure who, apart from being the long time leader of Rotherham MBC, was also the current Chair of the AMA, the national association of Metropolitan (including London Boroughs) Authorities. Another new Vice-President in

1991 was Gordon Gallimore, the Leader of Doncaster MBC, who became a member of the SYTT Board in November 1994 when he had retired from the Leader's position.

In 1993, Mark Beecroft replaced Frank Dever as Training Manager, with Elaine Sarson appointed to the new post of Senior Administrative Officer, and she reported straight to the Board on the school's administration and accounts. As part of the policy to raise the standards of the management of staff, and because the TEC were likely to make it mandatory before grants could be awarded in the near future, the School sought IiP (Investment in People) status in 1993, but this took a long time to process and was only finally awarded in December 1996. In the School's IiP submission, their mission statement, *"To become the best racing training school in Europe"* raised a few eyebrows in certain quarters, but it suited the new found confidence at Rossington Hall, after they had been put through the close scrutiny of the Struthers Working Party and the accountant's report and had emerged vindicated.

This confidence was reflected in the launch of a new logo in June 1994 and the confirmation that the colours of the NRS would be purple and green (the colours of the former SYCC). These would be used in all their promotional literature and on the new exhibition stands which their PR consultants, Colbear Dixon, had designed for use in recruiting trainees and sponsors at venues such as the Great Yorkshire Show.

The new logo incorporated a more stylised version of the previous logo and was first used with the words Northern Racing School. After a year this was changed to the format shown above after the final change of name in 1995.

In September 1995 there was another, and so far the final, change of name. The initial suggestion was advanced to aid recruitment. The school-leaving peers of NRS Trainees were all going to "college", having put "school" behind them, and so it was felt that replacing the School's name with College would make NRS more attractive, even more "cool", to young people. This in turn would encourage a growth in numbers, especially as the NRS now had to run courses for 120 trainees each year to meet RTBTB requirements. There was no opposition to the change of name, as all felt that **Northern Racing College** had a prestigious ring to it and suited the College's new sense of achievement.

Trainees exercise their horses in the yard of the Victorian Stables under the watchful eye of a TV camera crew.

Cantering Along

NRC 1996-2001

By the middle of the Nineties the NRC no longer felt it was under threat of closure through the financial rug being pulled from under it; instead it now felt free to continue to build on its strengths. Its main concern now was for more parity of opportunity with the BRS, in terms of the number of courses it was allowed to run by the BHB or the Jockey Club. Never short of ambition or hard graft, throughout the College's history it has been the College *"that never closed"*. There were always some trainees on site every day of the year, including Christmas Day, and the College has never had formal holidays like other educational institutions. Woodrow Wyatt, the former MP and Chairman of the Tote, once described them as *"the hard working school, the grafters"*, and this attitude had so far seen them overcome all obstacles and continually raise their standards and improve their facilities.

By the first half of 1996, NRC had 120 trainees on its books, with 31 horses in the stables and during that period past and present students had had 570 rides in public, including 53 winners, thereby demonstrating the continuing rise in standards at the College. Mark Beecroft had refined the training programme and restored the twelve-week cycle of courses, taking more trainees from trainers' yards, recruiting older trainees and streaming trainees according to ability. He had run a course the year before for amateur flat riders and a conditional (NH) jockeys' course, both courses run with the help of Ronnie Beggan, the former top National Hunt jockey. Always conscious of safety and fitness, in early 1996 the College had agreed to purchase skull caps for all the trainees. Three years later they went one further and decided that body protectors must be worn by all trainees on the initial course, because many of the injuries to the riders were back injuries. For a decade there had also been a rigorous P.E. programme, introduced after visits made to the Irish and French Training Schools, where physical fitness was a major element of their courses. For eight years this programme was run by Eddie McCoy, who had been the Chief Fire Officer for South Yorkshire and in retirement, after a distinguished career in the Fire Service, he took on the P.E work at Rossington Hall. The discipline that he instilled through his tough circuit training methods may not have always been appreciated by new trainees, but it stood them in good stead (the fitter they were the less problems they would have if they had a fall) when they went out to work at the yards and when they had rides in public.

Mark Beecroft resigned from his post as Training Manager in February 1997, after securing a position as an Investigating Officer for the Jockey Club. His equestrian training responsibilities were taken on by Kevin Frost, who had been a Senior Training Instructor at the NRC since early 1991. Mark's departure allowed further rationalisation of the staffing structure, which eventually led two years later to the arrival of Paul Foster, after a thirty year career in the Army, as the General Manager dealing with all the day to day administrative work of the NRC.

Apprentice Championship

Since 1992, the NRC and the BRS at Newmarket had competed in a seven-venue series of apprentice races aimed at giving their new trainees rides in public. However, the new British Horseracing Board (BHB) became increasingly unhappy about the restricted nature of these events and after the 1997 series would sanction no more. Instead a new competition was arranged, which also included the Irish racing school, RACE, whereby points would be awarded to apprentices riding in any races, including professional ones, with a scoring system based on places achieved (10 for a win, 6 for second, 2 for third and 1 for a ride). In 1998 the Championship started and finished at Doncaster Racecourse and the first race was won by NRC's Kimberley Hart. At the end of the season she had amassed enough points to be the Champion Woman Rider and two other NRC trainees, Chris Cogan and Craig Carver, were also in the top ten in the Championship.

The Robin Hastings Memorial Trust

These races for apprentices were first sponsored, in the Nineties, by the Robin Hastings Memorial Trust Fund, which had been set up by the British Bloodstock Agency (BBA) to support the development of apprentice jockeys. Thanks to the interest of Major Johnnie Lewis, a trustee of the Fund and a director of the BBA, this Trust continued to sponsor the new arrangements after 1998. Later when the balance of the fund was running low, they used the remaining monies to purchase a superb gold-plated equestrian trophy to be competed for by European apprentices in a race organised by the European Association of Racing Schools (EARS). In the first two of these European races, in 2003 at San Rossare in Italy and in 2004 at Doncaster, the British team, including NRC riders, won the trophy.

There were other honours for Kimberley Hart and two other trainees from the NRC, Paul Fessey and Derek McGaffin, when they were selected to represent British apprentices in a European Apprentices Challenge Race at Baden-Baden in the Black Forest. Organised by the German Jockey Club in May 1998, it pitted the three Brits against apprentices from Ireland, France and Germany.

The previous year in June 1997, Fergal Lynch, a 19 year old from Londonderry, became the first graduate from NRC to ride out his claim. This meant that he had ridden the 95 winners necessary to no longer be eligible to claim an apprentice's weight advantage, and he did it in a race at Redcar on a horse appropriately named "Weetman's Weigh". Fergal's first win had been in July 1995 and his most impressive win was on Sheikh Mohammed's horse "Clerkenwell" in the Tote Ebor Handicap at York in 1996. The success of these young NRC trained riders demonstrated to the racing world the quality of the trainees turned out by the NRC.

Derek McGaffin (in centre with large single star on his colours) the winner of the Baden-Baden race in 1998 is presented with the trophy.

Glasgow born Derek had no idea what to do when he left school, casually picked up the NRC leaflet in his careers office and decided to give Rossington Hall a try. Like so many NRC trainees he had never sat on a horse before, and now he was winning a prestigious race in Europe, despite having to rush home to get the documents for a new passport so that he could compete abroad.

Dominic Elsworth

In March 1997 Dominic Elsworth joined the Foundation Course at the NRC and went on to be the College's most successful rider over fences. To date he has ridden over 250 winners and competed in five Grand Nationals. Unlike many trainees who have no experience of horses when they come to Rossington Hall, Dominic, who was born in Guiseley in West Yorkshire, had been involved with horses all his life. He was working at the stables of Sue and Harvey Smith, when he had to do the course at Rossington Hall because of the new Jockey Club rules that required all under19s to get formal training. Despite this, Dominic found his time at the NRC useful and a good experience and shortly after leaving he got his licence in 1997.

His first ride was in December 1997 at Market Rasen, where he fell off, and he had to wait until February 1999 for his first winner, Moonshine Dragon, at Catterick. Since then he has had consistently successful seasons including winning the Becher Chase at Aintree in 2002 over the National fences, the Peter Marsh Chase at Haydock and the Castleford Chase at Wetherby.

A bewildering diversity of Funding

If finding the money to run the NRC had been complicated in the first decade of the Trust's existence it was about to get even more bewildering. There were so many potential sources of funding that it was like the old adage about the buses; if you missed one there would be another along in a few minutes. The money from the TEC dried up in the middle Nineties, after they were hit by a serious reduction in their funds from the Government, and they became reluctant to fund accommodation costs when trainees were out on placements far from South Yorkshire. So, for Government training funding the NRC now looked to a new partner, based in Dore in Sheffield. This private body, the National Training Partnership (NTP) had a contract, in best Thatcherite style, with the Government to deliver the funds for training for some of the largest organisations in the UK. Their clients included the Construction Industry Training Board, the Engineering Industry Training Board and Marks and Spencer, and although NRC was small potatoes alongside these organisations, NTP was prepared to take them on because the NRC's recruitment and placements now operated across Britain, and were no longer confined to their own county.

While the NTP funded the Level II and Level III NVQ training, the NRC managed to negotiate a new partnership arrangement to fund the Foundation Course, the "front end" training in the first twelve weeks for new trainees who were aiming to gain their Level I NVQ. From 1995-97, Doncaster College funded this part of the trainee costs because there was a financial advantage to them for "managing" another training franchise i.e. the NRC at Rossington Hall. They were prepared to pay £2400 for each trainee who completed the course but, in August 1997, the NRC managed to get a better deal from Grimsby College, based eighty miles away, and they took over the funding of the Foundation Course until 1999. Meanwhile other F.E. colleges such as Rother Valley, Bishop Burton near Beverley, Barnsley College and Sheffield College all showed an interest in funding the NRC at one time or another.

Then in May 1998 the NRC netted a very big fish in the form of a huge grant from the European Social Fund (ESF). Under their Objective 3 Programme, to help quality projects that would combat unemployment, the EU grant aided NRC to the tune of £148,494 for 1998, with the money from Grimsby College and the RTBTB being considered as matching funds, a requirement of ESF funding. They made a similar grant in 1999 and in 2000 their grant was worth £271,000 and ran till June 2001. This level of grant eased financial worries for the present and made some expansion possible, although it did cause some clawback of monies from Doncaster College, who claimed that there was some "double counting" with the ESF money, although the complicated rules had not been explained to the NRC. Doncaster College had restarted funding the Foundation Course in 2000 and they continued to do so until 2004.

In 1996 the College received a "Letter of Agreement" from the RTBTB and this allowed £112,000 funding to be given by them on behalf of the racing industry. To add to the complications they changed their name in 1998, when Sandy Struthers stood down as their Chairman (he accepted an invitation to become a Vice-President of NRC), and for a time they were known as the British Horseracing Training Board (BHTB) until they later became the British Horseracing Education and Standards Trust (BHEST). Thus, in the second half of the Nineties, the NTP, the F.E. Colleges at Doncaster and Grimsby and the BHTB were the main revenue funders, until it all changed again in 2001 with the arrival of the Learning and Skills Council (LSC). This initiative from David Blunkett's Education Department, was an attempt by the Labour Government to give some unity and cohesion to the somewhat chaotic funding system, by having one channel for government funding for Post-16 education and training, including academic sixth form "A" Level work at LEA schools across the country.

With all these sources of money available the NRC now had an annual budget of around half a million pounds, and it is perhaps not surprising that in one year (1994-95) the NRC made a small surplus of £41,000 on its running costs. This money was immediately squirreled away into the Development Fund towards the costs of several other planned projects. There was also substantial help from Sir Graham Kirkland, now Lord Kirkland, the owner of the DFS furniture firm, who gave the NRC a generous donation of £20,000 to add to the Development Fund, and from the Doncaster Racing Forum from an event at Doncaster Racecourse in 2001.

How the Money was Spent

From the Budget for April 1996-March 1997

Staff	£217,816	44%
Trainees inc Lodging	£132,100	27%
Rent and Repairs	£30,500	6%
Stable Costs inc feed	£39,000	8%
Facilites, e.g Gallop	£4,700	1%
Administration	£63,395	13%
Total	£ 487,511	100%

Tim Lyle, the new TGWU Board member, also suggested that an approach should be made to the Totalisator Board (the Tote) to see if they could release the money from unclaimed bets to help training and trainee accommodation costs, as happened in France with the Paris Mutuel betting system. The approach did not succeed, nor did appeals to the Sports Council for Lottery money for the residential block, or appeals to the Millennium Commission, who were bankrolling, with Lottery money, significant projects across the UK to celebrate the birth of a new century.

Paddy Aspell

Another successful National Hunt jockey who graduated from the NRC is Patrick "Paddy" Aspell. Paddy, born in Dublin, started at the College in 1999 after he came over from Ireland, where he had been riding horses since he was twelve years old and already had some race experience as an amateur jockey. "I really enjoyed my time at the NRC and found it very useful. I learned a lot about nutrition, fitness and various other areas of racing, including how to present myself to trainers"; he says.

After the NRC, Paddy started to get more rides and rode his first winner (as an amateur) in 2000, before turning conditional in 2001. In 2002 he rode in the Cheltenham Festival and has now ridden around 120 winners. 2006 was his best year yet when he rode 28 winners, and occasionally he rides abroad including a recent win in Italy. Like many former NRC trainees, he thinks himself lucky that he gets paid for doing a job he loves so much. His aim is to beat his personal best each season, keep free of injury and continue working hard to improve as both a jump and flat jockey.

The Indoor Riding School at last

With the Ninety-nine Year Lease finally signed at the beginning of 1996, the College could more confidently approach potential financial supporters, with appeals for capital grants to build the Indoor Riding School. There was a short-lived disappointment when the Sports Council did not support the scheme and therefore blocked Lottery money, but it was not a disappointment for long. The Levy Board, long a supporter of the NRC, came in with a 100% grant in April 1996. This made £240,000 available for the project and enabled the NRC to commission the builders, Pearsons, to get on and build the indoor school. It was finished in November 1996 and comprised a 60 x 40 metre riding area that would meet all of the College's requirements. Initially there was no viewing gallery but this was added in 2005 with a grant of £5000 from the Racing Post.

The official party at the opening of the new Indoor Riding Centre in January 1997.
   Left to right: Jim Gale, Lord Scarbrough, Colin Wedd, Coun. Dorothy Layton JP, the Mayor of Doncaster, and Sir John Sparrow, Chairman of the Levy Board.

Thirty guests witnessed the opening ceremony on 24th January 1997, performed, most appropriately, by Sir John Sparrow, the Chairman of the Levy Board, with Colin Wedd, riding round the arena, with some brio, to make the first official circuit of the building. One of the first benefits of the new facility was a winter programme of dressage and show jumping events, starting in October and running until March 1998.

Setting up the Trading Company

As SYTT was a charity it could not trade to make a profit. Yet, the facilities offered opportunities for making money and there were obvious benefits from having your own shop on the site (producing NRC's own Christmas cards was an early suggestion) and returning some percentage of the profits back into the Trust's funds. So in September 1997 the Board agreed to set up a trading company with its own separate board, but as a wholly owned subsidiary of the main SYTT Board. The suggestion for the size of the new trading company's board was six members, with as many as five being drawn from the current membership of the SYTT board. There were suggestions that Lord Zetland, who was the Chairman of Redcar Racecourse and had supported the Apprentice Racing Series, might be invited to join the board, or Barry Bruce of Furniture Factors Ltd, who was one of the Friends of NRC and could bring retail expertise to the new board's decisions.

   In the event Barry Bruce became the business partner on the new board, who at first thought of calling themselves *Rossington Hall Trading Company* to emphasize their separateness from SYTT, but in the end it was decided that this would confuse customers and users, and so they settled for the more mundane *"NRC Trading Ltd."*. They could not start trading till they had all the necessary documents from Companies House, and so the start was delayed well into the New Year, until the company's memorandum and articles of association were finally approved in the summer of 1998. By the end of the year a shop had opened at the College for the purchase of goods by the trainees at competitive prices. The new company operated a kind of truck system, in which the trainees were given £50 vouchers (later raised to £150) with which to make their purchases and the system worked satisfactorily, partly because the College was so far from the nearest village shops. Business was brisk and the setting-up costs were recovered by February 1999 and they were trading at a profit after one year. They handled all bookings and hire charges for the facilities and even considered growing their own hay and marketing it for feed. Originally they intended to give 25% of the profits back to SYTT but things were going so well (£50,000 turnover in the first year) that they raised it to 80%, with the other 20% going into a working capital fund. They even ran a fundraising Golf Day, always a useful earner, in Autumn 1999 at Wheatley Hall G.C. and among the golfers were A.P.McCoy, the 2007 Champion NH jockey and Andrew Thornton. With the help of other initiatives, the Trading Company continued to raise their turnover and consequently their contribution to the main SYTT Board's funds.

Expanding range of courses

During the period that Kevin Frost was the Training Manager, the number of students reached 140, the highest level yet, although not all of them completed the course. To save money, in 1998 the front-end Foundation Course was reduced to ten weeks, but the later part of the course now had to meet the requirements of the new Modern Apprenticeship, which not only included Level II NVQs, but also key skills courses in Literacy and Communication, Numeracy and IT. Trainees spent a quarter of their time in the classroom receiving theory lectures, and a pass at Level 1 NVQ was equal to GCSE grades D-G and at Level 2 to GCSE grades A-C, equivalent to the old "O" Level pass.

Not all students found this part of the course amenable and some dropped out. It was enough of a concern to the NRC for the Board to write to the Secretary of State for Education and Employment, David Blunkett, suggesting a reconsideration of the requirements.

The College found itself frustrated that it could not expand the range of courses, as it would have liked. A BHB Report in 1998, "The Future Structure of Training in the Horseracing Industry", accepted the need for two racing training institutions, but suggested that the majority of the advanced courses should go to the BRS, not the NRC. This failure to recognise true parity of opportunity between the two institutions continued to annoy and frustrate the NRC, as the BHB and the Jockey Club continued to restrict them over the number and type of courses they were allowed to provide. The

Zoe Horne

Zoe Horne came to the NRC in 1996 somewhat reluctantly. She had to take the Foundation Course under the new rules of racing (if you were under nineteen and wanted to gain a stable pass), although she had been riding ponies in the Cotswolds since she was three, and riding racehorses since she was eleven. Having completed the twelve-week course at Rossington Hall, she was fortunate to be employed by Venetia Williams in Herefordshire and later moved on to be pupil assistant to David Murray-Smith. In 1998 she became his assistant, gained her amateur jockey's licence, and rode in flat races during 1999 and 2000. In September 2002 she returned to Rossington Hall as a Quality Assurance Officer, but after eleven days her "gift of the gab" landed her the new post of Marketing and Recruitment Officer. Currently she lives on the site at the College, and believes she does an eighteen-hour day, seven days a week.

Board could still get very touchy about perceived snubs, as when the Jockey Club Report of 1999-2000 indicated that Malcolm Wallace, the Director of Regulation at the Jockey Club was visiting the BRS on a monthly basis whereas his visits to the NRC were considerably more infrequent.

Despite all this, new courses were started at the College by the beginning of the new century. There was a three week course for selected students run with the help of George Duffield, a former St. Leger winning jockey and Tim Reed, a former N.H. jockey, which included a week in Ireland at RACE and ended with a mock race at Southwell Racecourse run "in accordance with the Rules of Racing". There was a short course for Doncaster Bloodstock Sales staff, for which the TEC paid 50% of the costs, and an Apprentice and Conditional Jockey course, two important advanced courses that have continued to be run up to the present.

Bob Champion, possibly one of the few National Hunt jockeys known to the non-racing public, because of his great success on Aldaniti in the 1981 Grand National and his brave and successful fight against cancer (chronicled in the film of his life, where he was portrayed by John Hurt), also helped out with these courses, although he was initially retained by the College, in 2000, on a short term basis to help recruitment. His charisma and fame were certainly enough to boost recruitment and he seemed to enjoy his time at Rossington Hall, staying on until 2005.

A new departure in 2000 was a pilot course for schoolchildren aged 14-16 in Years 9,10 and 11. It ran for a day a week over a two year period and two of the first schools to undertake it were the local Rossington High School and, more surprisingly, Kingswood School in Hull, whose pupils came over from the East Riding on a regular basis to take part. In 2007 this course is still going strong, At the same time contact was made with the Young Offenders Institution at near-by Hatfield, to take a small number of ex-offenders on the NRC's Foundation Course. The College offered two places per course and, although the take up has been patchy, the NRC has had a number of young men from Hatfield, and also from Wetherby YOI (where Sandy Young, the SYTT Trustee, was a senior member of staff), with these trainees being bussed in every day for instruction at Rossington Hall. A few have subsequently, on release, taken up apprenticeships in trainers' yards and entered the industry.

Increasing International Connections

Right from the earliest days in 1984, the College, then SYARTS, had made a useful contact with the Irish training school, RACE, at the Curragh. These contacts had been widened in the next fifteen years and an international working party representing four countries had been set up in 1995 to continue the mutual co-operation. There were increasing contacts with the French AFASEC and with the Italian ALFEA company at Pisa, where the racing training facility was situated within a regional country park of 22,000 hectares, and in 1997 Colin Wedd was invited to speak to a conference at Merano in Alto Adige, about the progress being made at Rossington Hall. When he retired as the Director of the French racing training and social welfare centre, AFASEC, in 2000, Didier Garnier accepted an invitation to become a Vice President of the NRC. It was Didier Garner and the AFASEC who created a European Racing Qualification, the FELAJOC, in consultation with the NRC, RACE and the British Horseracing Training Board (BHTB).

This prestigious qualification, now called EQUES (the European Qualification for Employees in Stables) was designed to enable stable staff to work across the EU, and incorporated some aspects of the British NVQ Level II with the equivalent French BEPA. One of its additional features was that it demanded proficiency in one major foreign European language. This proved something of a stumbling block for NRC candidates, who, unlike young Europeans who often welcome learning English as the international language, had little practice or interest in foreign languages. A course to instruct candidates in French or Italian was devised at Middleham and eventually, in 2001, four NRC young ladies were successful in passing the FELAJOC, after being subjected to rigorous language tests in either French or Italian.

This qualification now came under the administration of the new formal association of these training institution partners. In 2000 they established the European Association of Racing Schools, comprising the NRC (UK), AFASEC (France), RACE (Republic of Ireland) and ALFEA (Italy) with the Direktorum, the German Jockey Club, attending as observers. They held one of their first meetings at Rossington Hall in June 2001, and in 2002 began the practice of a rotating chairman, with Derek O'Sullivan, who sadly died in office, voted in as the first Chairman, to be replaced by Dr. Stefano Meli of ALFEA (2003-04) and later Jim Gale (2005-06) held the post. In January 2007, Didier Budka of AFASEC became the current Chairman.

New Dreams – an Equestrian Country Park

Right from the very first days at Rossington Hall it had struck the Trustees that the Victorian Stables were situated in a superb rural setting, with an imposing 19th Century country house and the often hidden remains of its once great gardens. These included an overgrown Italian garden, not obvious to the casual observer, but one that provided reminders of the splendour that once existed. Jim Gale, in particular, long harboured the view that when the College had established itself, attention should be turned to planning, and eventually creating, a great country park themed around equestrian activity.

Colin Wedd (right) became Chair of Doncaster Racecourse in 1997 and was Leader of Doncaster MB Council between 1998-2001. As Chair of SYTT and also Chair of the NRC and Country Park Sub-Committees and NRC Trading Ltd., he has played a major part in the success of the College over a quarter of a century, and continues to guide its vision for the future.

A strong believer in the international dimension of the racing training world, he was a strong supporter of the foundation of EARS in 2000. In the photo above he is seen with Derek O'Sullivan, the Director of RACE in Kildare in Ireland, a staunch friend and supporter of the NRC over many years and the first Chairman of EARS 2001-2002.

The official local plan for the Doncaster District (the Unitary Development Plan) in the early Nineties, had identified Rossington Hall, and its surroundings, as a possible country park, to redress the lack of public open space in the south Doncaster area. So when Jim Gale drew up a Master Plan for a 253 acre country park in 2000, the Planning Department at Doncaster MBC included a written endorsement of his ideas. This was significant and important because it was the Borough's land that was under consideration. They did, however, indicate that there were other plans for the area; including building a Parkway railway station on the M18. The other plans still included those of the private developer who was considering creating two, near-by, golf courses, one of them to PGA championship standard, which might have impinged on any future plans for a country park at Rossington. However, the Doncaster officers, took it to the relevant committee of their Council who gave it their blessing in April 2001. They also helped to identify £9,975 of SRB (Single Regeneration Budget) grant money that enabled further work to be done on the Master Plan, using the professional help of RMJM, an Edinburgh firm of architects and landscape architects, who had recently done some architectural work for Doncaster Racecourse. As detailed in a later chapter, the Equestrian Country Park, now renamed the St. Leger Horse and Country Park, is an idea still awaiting fulfilment, but the seeds were sown almost a decade ago and it is now one of the most exciting areas of future development for the SYTT Trustees.

Two cheers for the Inspection

In October 2000 the work-based training programme of the College was inspected by the Training Standards Council (TSC), the training equivalent of OFSTED. They did not include the courses that were closely supervised at Rossington Hall in their remit, but instead just wanted to inspect how the trainees were supervised when out in placements at the trainers' yards. This was not so easy to supervise by the College, because the final responsibility for how things were managed rested with the local staff at the yards, and they often had other priorities apart from supporting NRC trainees. However, it was felt that the inspection had gone well, but the subsequent report, while generally sympathetic, did have some basic criticisms and suggestions.

While recognising the valuable work by Laine Wakefield, the NRC's Monitoring Officer, who was responsible for the pastoral care of trainees when away from Rossington Hall on placement, they did feel that there were measures that could be taken to improve training in the work place. These included proposals that there should be more "off the job" training sessions, to allow increased discussion by trainees of their work experiences in the trainers' yards and when taking horses to races. The report also indicated a need for better assessment procedures by the NRC while trainees were out on placement.

Most organisations when they receive some criticism from an official outside agency, often become very defensive, but a well-run inspection should be viewed as a valuable appraisal by a new pair of eyes and a genuine attempt to improve standards. So, the NRC drew up an Action Plan to take on board all of the TSC's points, though shortly afterwards the TSC, like many a quango, was abolished, a regular feature of British public life, and replaced by the Adult Learning Inspectorate (ALI). By the next inspection in 2001 the NRC was judged to be a success, with improved grades in each of the areas inspected. In 2006 the ALI delivered another report praising the outstanding work of the College and citing it as one of the "Best of the Best" among all the various training institutions in the U.K.

Paul Foster has been the General Manager since 1999 and has responsibility for all things administrative at the NRC.

Paul Foster joined the NRC from the Army in October 1999 after thirty years service, latterly with Army Recruitment in Nottingham. Doncaster born, he was the son of a soldier and served in his father's successor regiment. His father had served in the 7th Queen's Own Hussars which amalgamated with the 3rd Kings Own Hussars in 1958 to form the Queen's Own Hussars, the regiment that Paul joined in 1972 after two and a half years at the Junior Leader's Regiment at Bovington.

Although the Queen's Own Hussars was a cavalry regiment it had long ago swopped horses for tanks, and Paul did his service on Chieftain and Challenger tanks, the British Army's main battle tanks of the period. Therefore, Paul had not ridden a horse during his time in the Army, although the officers of the regiment did keep horses, and so he was not entirely unfamiliar with them when he arrived at the NRC. After joining the Army at 15 years of age, he joined his regiment in Germany at 17 and worked through the ranks until he was appointed Regimental Sergeant Major in 1991 in the rank of Warrant Officer, Class One. In 1993 he was selected to join the Army's Long Service List and worked with Army Recruitment, based in Leeds and then Nottingham, until he retired from the Army in 1999, when he took up his present post at the NRC.

The Finningley Interlude 2000-03

It took Paul Foster, the new General Manager, nearly twelve months to learn how the NRC operated, but his Army experience organising people and events, as well as training recruits fitted in well with the requirements of his new post. One of his early tasks was to set up the temporary residential accommodation at Finningley, the former RAF airbase, now the Robin Hood Airport. The redundant RAF buildings had been re-commissioned to accommodate refugees from the war in Kosovo, and when they left, the facilities, which had by then had some considerable investment spent on them, appeared to offer an ideal stop-gap solution to the problem of residential accommodation for trainees.

There was absolutely no equipment in either of the two blocks that the NRC used. So, the College purchased all the basic furniture and equipment for the dormitory block, with the intention that it could all be moved to Rossington Hall when the residential block was finally completed. The other building used at Finningley had once been the Junior NCOs' Mess and served as the kitchens, dining and recreation room, and again all the cooking equipment had to be bought in with a specification that it would fit more permanent accommodation in the near future. For three years all trainees were housed at Finningley, after it had proved difficult to maintain an adequate roster of private landladies with digs conveniently sited for trainees to get to the College. Finningley was only a mile away and the trainees were bussed in daily by the College's new minibus. NRC took on the catering company EUREST to run the catering, while new staff, including Shirley Richards-Newton (who had been one of the landladies who looked after NRC trainees before Finningley) and Carol Fisher, were taken on to run the accommodation. They then moved across to Rossington Hall when the new residential block was ready in January 2003.

After Paul Foster had arrived at the College in 1999, one of his first jobs was to set up a new Computer Suite of eleven computers and a workstation situated in the library, thereby bringing up to date the IT equipment and increasing the teaching opportunities at the NRC. The suite was funded by a grant from the National Trainers' Federation's Charitable Fund and their Chief Executive, Sir John Kemble, a senior commander at Northwood during the Falklands War, was invited to open the facility. This helped to inspire the college's own website, set up in 2001, and generally to make all the trainees more computer literate.

"Caesar's Palace" under Starter's Orders

Finally, after almost two decades, the tenders went out in 2000 for the building of the Residential Accommodation. A new planning permission had to be obtained from Doncaster MBC because the plans had been altered as a result of a cost cutting exercise, although it was still budgeted to cost £1.3 million. Once this new planning permission was granted the Levy Board, who had long supported the scheme in principle, agreed its substantial grant of £250,000. Other major contributors included the Coalfields Regeneration Trust, whose funding came from the EU to aid areas devastated by the closure of coal mines. They chipped in with £200,000, and a huge personal donation of £100,000 was given by Sir Robert Ogden CBE, a Yorkshire millionaire, who owned a

Pictured here are "the Gang" including Danielle McCreery (in Headband). They were part of a group of trainees who started their course in residence at Finningley and then were the first residents of the new accommodation at Rossington Hall in 2003.

string of racehorses and had become a Vice President of the NRC a few months previously. The Single Regeneration Budget that channelled ESF money into South Yorkshire was prepared to offer £362,000 and the SYTT's own Development Fund, with money carefully garnered over the years from the Annual Charity Race Meetings at Pontefract, added £230,000. In the end there were several corporate contributors, including the Childwick Trust and the NTF CharitableTrust Fund and £120,000 from Doncaster MBC. There were also many smaller individual donors some of whom paid for a "brick": these, on completion of the building, were displayed on a wall in the entrance foyer, including one, seemingly rather improbably, from the Lord Mayor of Salford and others from football legends George Best, Kevin Keegan and Sir Alex Ferguson.

The tenders were returned in February 2001, and Hallamshire Construction, with a tender of £1,111,279 was selected from an invited list of seven companies, including some of the best known names in the local construction industry in South Yorkshire. In December 2001, Richard Caborn, the new Minister for Sport and Sheffield Central MP, ceremoniously turned the first sod to mark the beginning of the construction of a building that was long overdue and very much needed.

Richard Caborn, the Minister for Sport in Tony Blair's government, turns the first sod to start the construction of the new residential block. Colin Wedd holds a watching brief.

Paul Foster in a previous life as WO1 P. FOSTER, the Regimental Sergeant Major of the Queen's Own Hussars. Also featured on this painting, which was presented to Paul by the Warrant Officers and Sergeants' Mess on his retirement from the regiment, is Peninsular, the Regimental Drum Horse, named after Wellington's Iberian campaign and given to the regiment by their Colonel in Chief, the late Queen Mother.

Sharing the Lead

NRC 2002-07

During the last half decade the NRC has moved some considerable way to realising its current strapline *"to become the best racing college in Europe"*. The important milestones include the completion of the Residential Block in 2003, in effect two buildings because one wing houses reception, offices, a dining room, kitchen, meeting and recreational rooms, while the other wing houses the twenty-seven bedrooms and communal facilities used by trainees on the various courses. The completed building is such a good match with the 19th Century Victorian Stables that a casual observer might well initially think they were all constructed during the same period. In 2004 the Donoughue Report into the recruitment, training and conditions of stable and stud staff, served as a watershed for the NRC when it gave them a ringing endorsement, clearing the way for them to have parity with the BRS in the organising and running of specialist courses. Before Donoughue the NRC was never allowed to run more than eight different courses: now the figure is in excess of twenty and rising. In 2006 the ALI, having rigorously inspected the College in May, also delivered a verdict of "outstanding" on all aspects of the work at Rossington Hall, and later included them, along with the BRS, among the "Best of the Best" of the training institutions in the country. There has been more co-operation between the two horseracing schools in recent years, with joint marketing initiatives like "Feel the Buzz" to increase recruiting across the UK, and the BRS joining EARS, the European Association of Racing Schools, in 2004.

If the core activity of the Trust at Rossington Hall, i.e. the NRC and NRC Trading, is on very firm foundations, then there has been increasing thought given to the vision of what could be achieved on an expanded site. The Equestrian Country Park plans have cautiously evolved, with some elements including the two trainers' stables and a second gallop already a reality. The plans for the Country Park are as breathtaking as they are ambitious. They could one day include Rossington Hall itself as a new land-based college, like Bishop Burton in the East Riding or Askham Bryan, near York. The decade has already seen plans to widen the NRC's influence to work with partner colleges in Lancashire, Wiltshire and other English regions, to deliver horserace training courses, and a considerable amount of effort was expended by the NRC on setting up a Scottish Racing Academy in the Lothian Region, which for the moment appears to be on hold.

The new Residential Block, including reception, offices, meeting rooms, kitchen and dining room as well as 27 rooms for trainees, opened for business in January 2003, with the formal opening by Princess Anne in November of that year. Paul Brookes, who had done much of the design work on the refurbished Victorian Stables in the Eighties, was the architect who pulled off a superb match of the two main buildings of the College, which were actually built 120 years apart.

Assembling the new team

Despite the very pleasant environment at Rossington Hall and the well-motivated student body, there has always been a steady turnover of staff because of the opportunities open to experienced NRC employees. In 2007 the staff establishment numbers twenty-seven and for a time the technical staff were under a new Director, Mike Mason, who joined the NRC in August 2006 from the National Stud, after a distinguished career in the RAF Regiment.

In 2002 the College acquired a new logo – its Fifth. The striking design was produced by the NT Partnership's Design Department and was the focal point of NRC's new house style.

Mike was also an accomplished show jumper – the first RAF officer to compete at the Royal International Horse Show at Hickstead, and at the Royal Windsor Horse Show – but he left the NRC within a year, after experiencing travelling difficulties from his home in Essex. The administrative side continued to be led by Paul Foster, the General Manager, who has been at the NRC since 1999. In 2002 Zoe Horne, who had been a trainee herself at the NRC in 1996, became the first holder of the new post of Marketing and Recruitment Officer, while Joanne Ellis (née Beresford) came originally as a part-time Equestrian and Key Skills Instructor around the same time, but then took over the new post of Senior Quality Assurance Officer when the first holder of the post, Jane Smith (née Hindmarsh) left. In 2006 Joanne became the first Chief Education and Training Officer at the NRC. The position of Training Manager was left unfilled after 2002, but Steve Goodings arrived and served as Chief Instructor, with Paul Foster acting as line manager for all the technical (horse-training related) staff until 2006. When Steve left in 2006, Malcolm Bygrave, who had been in the second group of trainees in 1984 at, what was then called, SYARTS, moved up into the Chief Instructor's position and in June 2007 he became the new Training Manager when the post was re-established after Mike Mason left. NRC Trading's two Commercial Managers, Ian Yates and then Ben Mico, have built up the trading arm of the Trust so that today its turnover is over £250,000, with an annual contribution to the Trust of over £80,000.

In 2007 there are also three full-time Quality Assurance Officers who cover different parts of the country, assessing the progress of NRC trainees when they are out on placement. Kate McDermott works out of London and covers NRC trainees in yards in the South of England, while Vanessa Cashmore visits yards in the North (including several at Middleham and Malton) and in Scotland. Georgie Sherry from Armthorpe, is the QAO who keeps an eye on trainees in the Midlands, and between them they cover 62 locations where NRC's trainees are presently under instruction and assessment.

A Royal Opening

Paul Brooke's superbly designed Residential Block, long promised (it had been in the development plans for almost twenty years) and important to the quality and coherence of the trainees' experience at Rossington Hall, was completed on time and on budget by Hallamshire Construction on 17th January 2003. Including fixtures and fittings it had cost £1.3 million, and after all the trainees and all the equipment had been transferred over from Finningley, it started business at the end of January 2003. Carol Fisher and Shirley Richards-Newton moved across as well and EUREST, whose staff at that time included Jean Jackson, were given the new catering contract. Paul Foster had acted as the Project Manager during the building period, working closely with Peter Dorman, a former SYCC quantity surveyor, who had been the development consultant for the Trust since 1996.

Carol Fisher is the Senior Residential Supervisor and, before she was recruited by the NRC to work at Finningley, she had been working for Care in the Community, looking after the elderly. Although born in Berkshire, she grew up in Doncaster and now swapped caring for one end of the age scale for the opposite end.

She claims her charges have been little problem over the years, unlike a huge eagle owl that took up residence near the buildings and practised its hooting about every four seconds. Nicknamed Betty, it was two feet high and had a wing span over six feet, attacking dogs and perching on the benches in the yard until it was persuaded to go and live elsewhere in December 2005.

Staff members working in the Residential Block have their own flats adjacent to the trainees' rooms and do a four-day on, four-day off rota. When on duty they are on call all night, but their official hours are 6.30-9.30 am and 4.00-11.00pm and so theoretically the daytime is their rest period.

The twenty-seven rooms were almost all twin bedrooms with basic, even spartan, furniture that included an open wardrobe and a portable TV. However, trainees were expected to be at work by 7.30 am, so they would not have too much time to admire the décor. Boys had the upper landing and girls the middle one, and trainees under 18 could not room with ones over 18 under the current Children Act legislation. Trainees on the Foundation Course are awakened at 6.30 am (the yards they are going to will all have early starts) but they can exercise an option on whether to have the self-service breakfast or sleep in for a bit longer.

The College thought they had it all teed up for the Queen to open the Residential Block. She was due to visit South Yorkshire in the autumn of 2003 and her motorcade would be passing down the Great North Road past the College on its way into Rotherham. This did not happen in the end because her schedule was judged to be too busy already, even though the Queen's police security

"Betty" on the roof guarding and terrorising all at the same time.

Princess Anne talks to staff and trainees during her visit to open the new residential block in 2003. Kate McDermott, the QAO, and Dawn Watson are the staff members in the centre of the photograph.

team had visited the NRC and checked it out for possible security problems. Instead it was Princess Anne, making her second visit to Rossington Hall, who did the honours on 27th November 2003, with Paul Foster running a flawless "parade" as befitted a former RSM of the Queen's Own Hussars.

The Donoughue "Liberation"

Few industries can have commissioned so many reports into their workings as the horseracing industry has done over the last two decades. However, an industry that is so diverse and disparate, and is the sixth biggest employer in the United Kingdom, needs to keep reflecting on its progress and its future. The Stable and Stud Staff Commission set up in July 2003 was better known by the name of its chairman, Lord Donoughue. Set up as an independent inquiry by the BHB, who wanted a fresh view of how recruitment, training and career development of stable and stud staff should be managed. Bernard Donoughue had operated at the highest political levels since, as a thirty-year-old in 1974, he had been plucked from a post as a lecturer at the London School of Economics to be one of Harold Wilson's closest policy advisers at No 10. He had a long time interest in racing, having been among other things a former Director of Towcester Racecourse and Chairman of the Starting Price Regulatory Board. The NRC was hopeful of a fair hearing from a man of his experience, especially one with impeccable left of centre credentials.

Jim Gale wrote the NRC's submission to the Commission, making a series of trenchant points about improving the marketing of opportunities available to potential

Danielle McCreery

Danielle McCreery, now a successful apprentice jockey with fifteen winners to her name, was in the first group that lived in the new residential block in 2003. She had started her course in the temporary accommodation at Finningley, but after two weeks she moved over to Rossington Hall with the rest of her course members. She was the only girl to finish the course in that group, and found the rigorous, even spartan life-style, to be a great shock to all the trainees, even those boys who thought they were tough and street-wise. She remembers she discovered groaning muscles she did not know she possessed and believes that, although the regime at Rossington Hall either made you or broke you, it was a "fantastic experience" that stood you in good stead when you went out to a trainers' yard.

In 2005 Danielle was chosen to represent Britain, along with another girl and two boys, in the European International Apprentice Race held in Ireland, racing against apprentices from the other training schools in Europe. In 2006 she won the prestigious Apprentice Racing Competition and her prize was the opportunity to ride for a trainer in South Africa for a month in 2007.

Born in Bradford, she had ridden ponies and horses as a girl, but until she chose to come on the course at the NRC she had expected her career to lie elsewhere, and was in fact working in a hotel.

Picture by Keith Robinson of Fotosport Ltd.

Danielle McCreery, a winner on Lysandra in the Betfair Series.

Like many others, who decided to try the Foundation Course at Rossington Hall, she persevered and now has a promising career as a flat jockey in horseracing.

recruits. The real concern of the NRC was that they had few specialist courses, currently only a one-week Apprentice Licence (Flat racing) Course and a Conditional (NH) Jockey's Course, and they questioned the policy of the Jockey Club and the BHTB that all new specialist courses should be delivered only by the BRS at Newmarket. These included courses for remedial training of jockeys, some of whom had to literally drive past the NRC to reach Newmarket from Yorkshire and further north. The NRC also made it clear that they would welcome the opportunity to establish a Jockeys' Academy at Rossington Hall as one very positive way of addressing the dearth of jockeys in Great Britain. *"In my opinion the two schools should be treated equally"* Jim Gale concluded and the Donoughue Commission agreed. In the Findings of their Report of July 2004 they said;

> *"Both the BRS and the NRC have impressed us in the course of our inquiry. However, the imbalance in the range of courses each is contracted to provide is striking."*

The upshot of this fairly measured statement was that the restrictions on the NRC were largely removed and during the next two years the courses on offer at the College more than doubled. All the Trustees and Staff recognise that the Donoughue Commission and their Report provided a seminal moment in the progress of the NRC, and an encouraging springboard to launch their ambitions for the future.

The Changing Scene

Not every finding of the Donoughue Report has been fully implemented as yet, but the BHB used the good offices of Baroness Mallalieu to ensure the implementation of its recommendations. She is a horseracing enthusiast, but as a barrister, recorder and former Labour Front Bench spokeswoman in the Lords, she was not the sort of person to be fobbed off with lame excuses and compromises. She visited the NRC in December 2004, claimed that she was impressed with what she saw, and resolved to make sure that there would be no going back on Donoughue's position on the issue of equality of opportunity for delivering courses. The previous history of who should be allowed to do what, was becoming irrelevant to the new faces in the horseracing establishment. Prominent among the movers for change was the new Duke of Devonshire, who, as Marquis of Hartington, had seen the need for the Jockey Club to relinquish many of its governance responsibilities to the BHB. He realised, even if some traditionalists did not, that, like the MCC's position in cricket, you could not have a private club running a huge international sport in the Twenty-First Century in Britain. More recently there were other people like Sara Hay-Jahans, the new Head of the BHB Recruitment and Training Department, who wanted to maximise the training courses available not just defend old investments, and the Minister of Sport, Richard Caborn, a product of the Sheffield steel industry unions, who had no time for old prejudices and new restrictive practices.

The new courses

After 2004 the numbers and types of course offered by the College expanded exponentially. Now there are over twenty courses covering amateurs, apprentices, conditional jockeys, assistant trainers, point to point riders, teenage pony riders, even the King's Troop of the Royal Horse Artillery. The latter group, all serving soldiers, came to Rossington Hall in 2006 to polish up their point-to-point skills, before competing in the Troop Race on the infamous Larkhill Course. They were put through an intensive one week course, by

Malcolm Bygrave and the NRC's jumping consultant, Tim Reed, using their own army horses who were more familiar with pulling guns on ceremonial occasions.

Tim Reid has also been involved in the massive overhaul of the Conditional Jockey's Course, where students school over fences every day, and then analyse their performance on video, which also enables them to look critically at the jumping techniques of different horses.

The BHB allowed the College to set up an Assistant Trainers' course in 2007, and also a Remedial Training course for Jockeys based in the North to enable them to keep up to scratch and up to date. There are now non-riders' courses aimed at other sections of the industry, like the Racing Secretaries' Course preparing students for the administrative side of racing with instruction in Employment Law, International Racing and the Rules of Racing, and familiarity with banking and online entries and declarations. One of the new courses, entitled the "Winning Formula", is a three-week long residential course aimed at university or college graduates who are considering entering the industry as a career. This course includes instruction in sports psychology, breeding of racehorses, pedigree analysis and racing administration. All this seems a far cry from the earliest days of SYARTS and the County Council, whose primary concern was getting unemployed young people, with limited educational qualifications, off the dole and into work – frankly any work!

Darasim is the star of the Rossington Hall stables. A former Goodwood Cup winner in 2004 trained by Mark Johnston, he was retired by his Swiss owner and came to the NRC at the end of 2006. Now nine years old, Darasim had 11 wins from 45 starts and earned £350,000 in prize money during his career on the track. Described by one NRC staff member as; "a horse that gives NRC trainees an experience like driving a Ferrari rather than a Ford or a Vauxhall, when they take Darasim out for a ride".

Hayley Turner, in centre of picture along with team mate Andrew Mullen, receiving the EARS Trophy, donated by the Robin Hastings Memorial Trust, from Major Johnnie Lewis (left) at the EARS Championship Race at Doncaster 2004.

Hayley Turner

Hayley Turner is possibly the best known graduate of the NRC. She came to Rossington Hall for the Foundation Course in August 1999 and completed her NVQ Level 2 in October 2000. Before coming to the NRC she had learnt to ride at her mother's riding school near Southwell. Clearly she was a very talented rider who was going to make an impression on the sport in a very short time. She got rides with leading trainers like Luca Cumani and Henry Cecil at Newmarket, and more recently Richard Hannon at Marlborough. Newmarket trainer Martin Bell, who trained Motivator, the 2005 Derby winner, has shown faith in her ability and in 2005 she became the joint Champion Apprentice along with Saleem Golam with 44 winners apiece. Many of the great names of British racing have held this title, including Lester Piggott, Pat Eddery and Frankie Dettori, and her success marks her out as a top jockey of the future. In 2006 she won the award of "Female Jockey of the Year", another step towards changing perceptions of women jockeys on the English racing circuit.

It is Zoe Horne's task to recruit for all these courses and among her targets is keeping a gender balance, currently 60-40 in favour of females, and also encouraging Black and Ethnic Minority (BME) youngsters to come on to the courses. Women jockeys regularly get a ride in public but they are still very much a minority on the track, and there is little tradition among BME youngsters of going into racing, but it will happen. Remember, that was said about golf before Tiger Woods, and about Formula One before Lewis Hamilton. To emphasise the point in 2005 the Champion Apprenticeship was shared, on 44 wins each, between NRC's own Hayley Turner and Saleem Golam, who trained at the BRS.

The Loyal Friends of NRC

Sue Gale (left) Secretary of the Friends of NRC, and Stancee Wedd, the current Chair, share a joke after a meeting of the Friends, where they have been planning how to raise more money for the College.

Since their first events in 1989 the Friends of the NRC had run regular fund-raising events, particularly the Open Days in September and the Race Night in the Spring, and every year they also provided practical help at the Charity Race Day at Pontefract, all of which contributed to the SYTT's income to the tune of around £5,000 per annum. Now numbering sixty members, they had devised the "Wall of Names" to aid the fundraising for the Residential Block, and produced the first NRC Christmas card, which proved to be such a best seller. Indeed, the painting that was used on the Christmas cards, had originally been donated to the College by the Friends. In November 2003 they handed over £9000, their best contribution to date and it was a fitting tribute to the efforts of Mike Burns, who had been their Chairman for fourteen years, who now decided to stand down. He accepted an invitation to become a Vice-President, but now directed his enthusiasm back into the political arena and at the age of eighty-nine became the Mayor of Hatfield in 2006. His place was taken by Stancee Wedd, who had played a large part in the Friends over the years, as had Sue Gale, who had been the Secretary from the early days of the group. Paul Wilson, a NatWest bank manager, and Andrea Mallinson continued as Treasurer and Membership Secretary respectively. They started a new fundraising scheme with a "Walk of Names" modelled on the "Path of Fame" they had seen at Old Trafford. It was another way to buy a small piece of immortality by purchasing a brick, inscribed with one's name, that would be part of a path that would eventually stretch between the new building and the Victorian Stables. As this was a fair distance it was a scheme that could run for years, unlike the "Wall of Names" in the reception area that could only occupy a finite amount of space.

Andrea Mallinson served as the Friends' Membership Secretary between 2000-07. It was her idea to appeal for funds for the new residential building by offering bricks for sale that would contain the donor's name and form a wall in the reception area. She also initiated the "Walk of Names", which is an ongoing way of raising financial support for the College. Her husband, Chris Mallinson, is a Board member of the SYTT.

The Friends now became more ambitious, with trips to Prague in 2004, which took in the steeplechase racing at Pardubice and, in the following year, a visit to Paris to see the Grand Steeplechase of Paris at Auteuil, the French equivalent of the Cheltenham Gold Cup. Whilst in France they also met up with Hayley Turner, who rode a winner in one of the races they attended. In 2007 they were off to Merano in Northern Italy to see the Gran Premio Merano Forst, and at home they widened the scope of their events in 2006 with a successful wine tasting evening at the Wedd's home, Hampole Priory, and an Indian Buffet at a restaurant in Blyth. They also produced a newsletter in 2005 and, along with their general fundraising, they still found the opportunity to support some specific projects for the benefit of the trainees, when in 2005 they purchased an air hockey table for the Students' Recreation Room.

Seeking New Partners

The College after 2002 planned to extend its training activities by setting up courses at partner, or satellite, colleges in the UK. In Scotland, where there were no racing training schools, the College became even more ambitious and for four years tried to establish a Scottish Racing Academy in the Lothian Region. A lot of time and effort was expended on business plans and securing potential funders – Scottish Enterprise showed real interest – and it seemed that a dual centre Academy would be established at Oatridge College near Livingstone in West Lothian, and at the Woodlands Racing Stables at Dunbar in East Lothian. At Oatbridge, trainees would do a 13 week Foundation Course, managed by the NRC, before moving on to develop their practical skills at Dunbar. East Lothian Council was a firm supporter of this project and Musselburgh (previously Edinburgh) Racecourse was enthusiastic to see the Academy succeed. One or two of the SYTT Trustees were concerned that a Scottish Racing Academy might attract recruits who would otherwise come to Rossington Hall, but the Donoughue Report stressed the need for increased recruitment into the racing industry, and local colleges or local courses were one clear way to address the issue of the shortage of skilled staff.

The business plan for 2004-06 for the Scottish Racing Academy was approved by a management committee that was already in place, whose Chair was Norman Murray, the Leader of East Lothian Council, with Colin Wedd as Vice Chair. However, at that point the project went cold after the contract to secure the funding for the NVQ's Level 1 was arranged with Scottish Enterprise. Similarly, there has been limited progress with a scheme to widen the NRC's remit in England. Named the Five College Project, the aim was to replicate the Scottish Academy plan in five regions of England. The colleges who were in discussion with the NRC included Myerscough College, near Preston, Wiltshire College, covering the South West, Plumpton College (South East) and Moulton College in Northamptonshire to serve the Eastern counties, with Warwickshire College at

Moreton Morrell covering the West Midlands. The only course that has got off the ground so far is the Level 1 Foundation Course for equine studies students at Wiltshire College on their Lackham campus. The plan is for the colleges to serve as the regional centre for Level 1 Courses (nine weeks in the region and the last three weeks at Rossington Hall) with the NRC administering the quality of the training at the "satellite" colleges, before the trainees return to Rossington Hall to do the final part of their Level 1 course and enrol on the Level 2 course and, hopefully, their NVQ Level 3 eventually.

Trainers on Site

Another new departure for the College was the development of facilities for trainers to become tenants and work on site at the NRC. Among the advantages to the College would be the opportunity for trainees on the Foundation Course to see what went on in a trainer's stables and to be a feature, even active participant, in the future Country Park. To this end two magnificent stable blocks, designed by RMJM in an appropriate horseshoe shape, were constructed close to the Grey Barn in 2003. Hallamshire Construction did the building work under a partnering agreement and SRB money provided £300,000, which covered 75% of the costs. Included in the building project was the conversion of rooms over the swimming pool in the yard of the Victorian Stables, which were turned into three separate bed-sit flats for use by trainers for their staff's accommodation.

The first trainer moved into one of the stables in 2004, after other trainers had used the gallop and facilities earlier. Now, the trainer on site is Jimmy O'Reilly, a flat racing trainer, who initially had the use of one stable but after returning in August 2006, has occupied both stables where he looks after thirty horses. There are plans to extend the area by building a third stable, designed around a circular yard that replicates the curving shape of the Victorian Stables and two new horsewalkers were installed in June 2007. They can handle five horses at a time and one is the property of Jimmy O'Reilly, while the other replaces the old four horse machine that the NRC had used since 1993.

An American Legend

In September 2005, Chris McCarron, one of the greatest jockeys ever to grace the US tracks, and a Hall of Fame inductee, visited the NRC on a fact finding mission to share ideas that will enable him to open a new racing academy in Lexington KY. His target is to turn out twenty jockeys a year at his new academy, where he has been joined by Steve Cauthen who has become one of the trustees. It was something of an honour to host the visit of a man who rode 7141 winners in his 28-year career and he, in return, was impressed by what he saw. "Fantastic facilities and a great programme to go with it." He told the NRC staff members before he returned to the States.

Jimmy O'Reilly, second from left, with two of the horses he has under training, in front of the new horseshoe shaped stable blocks at Rossington Hall.

Continued Success of the Trading Company

The trainers, their stables and the accommodation are all managed by the NRC Trading Limited, the company set up in 1998 to handle all of SYTT's commercial operations. The intention then was that more income could be generated from the College's facilities and equipment, including promoting the potential for "covering" mares by the NRC's stallion, Daawe, and for breeding from the three broodmares in residence, Feiticeira, Chichen Itza and Kandymal.

This could lead to a thoroughbred-breeding course in the near future. Among the items that make up the revenue earning ability of the Trading Company are livery charges for owners' horses cared for in NRC's stables, and local events such as the Doncaster Show, the East Pennine Polo Crosse matches, and the East Midlands Dressage Group's competition. The Trading Company continues to make haylage for the College and private clients, and through the work of their two maintenance supervisors, John Hemlock and Steve Fisher, they take responsibility for maintaining the land and property of SYTT.

Comings and Goings

During the Nineties the SYTT Board of Management had been fairly stable, but in the new Century, there was something of a sea change in the membership, although the quality of the membership remained high and supportive in a practical way that would be the envy of most boards of directors. In 2004 Roy Thwaites stood down when he moved to

Daawe, the NRC's resident stallion has been in the College stables since the end of 2000. Born in the USA in 1991, he won 17 races between 1993 and 2000. His last race was at Southwell in December 2000 after which he was retired to Rossington Hall. He is seen here with Ray Petersen, who is an instructor at the NRC and hails from New Zealand.

Since February 2006 the Trading Company has been led by its Commercial Manager, Ben Mico, an Australian from Sydney NSW. After completing his Physical Education Degree Course at the Australian College of Physical Education, at Olympic Park, Sydney, he came to Britain, where he did his teaching practice at Mount St. Mary's College, the independent school at Spinkhill, not far from Rossington Hall. They offered him a full-time post for one year and he set up their new Leisure Club, which is a dual-use facility for use by the school and the public. When his visa expired in 1998, he went back to Australia and worked for two years in the Intercontinental Hotel's Leisure Club in Sydney. Returning to the U.K. in 2000, he went back to Mount St. Mary's College and ran the Leisure Club he had previously established. He became the new Commercial Manager of NRC Trading Ltd. after Ian Yates, his predecessor, moved on.

The People's Race 2007

Another new initiative involving the NRC is the People's Race run at Aintree on the day of the Grand National. The idea is to give novice riders, even non-riders, a chance to get first class intensive training and then ride a six-furlong flat race in front of thousands of race-goers on the big day at Aintree.

3500 hopefuls applied and eventually thirty were selected for training at the NRC and the BRS. They were a mixed bunch, including a housewife, a fire fighter, a bricklayer and office workers and their ages ranged between twenty and forty. Malcolm Bygrave organised the 16-day training regime for fifteen aspirant jockeys at the College, starting in February. On 14th April, with almost 70,000 people looking on, ten of the riders took part in the race that was the first race on the card on Grand National day. None of the NRC trained riders got a place. However, the true importance of the occasion is in taking part and representing all those who dream of riding, in what is probably, horseracing's greatest day of the year anywhere in the world.

The ten "People's Race" jockeys wait nervously for the moment when they went out on to the course at Aintree on 14th April 2007

Blackpool and his position as Vice Chair was taken by Howard Wright. Both men have played a key role in the history of the NRC, with Roy able to claim he was one of the "midwives" of the project back in 1982. Howard, as Associate Editor of the Racing Post, has probably as much inside knowledge of the racing industry as anyone and this has been vitally useful to the College, especially in its fledgling days.

Howard Wright was born in Doncaster in 1945 and educated at Doncaster Grammar School. His interest in racing was fired at an early age when he was taken by his family to the local racecourse. He has seen every St. Leger since 1948, even if the early ones were viewed from the shoulders of his grandfather when he was too young to remember the Classic race. His appointment as a trustee of the NRC in 1990, brought his involvement with Rossington Hall a full circle, because he remembers visiting the hall and the grounds with a party from his junior school on a day trip, long before anyone had the idea of using the stables as a training school.

Howard's hobby turned into an unexpected career as a racing journalist, after he had initially, for a brief period, been a civil servant. Among the posts he has held there was a period as deputy sports editor on the Sheffield Morning Telegraph, and later deputy racing editor of the Daily Telegraph, which caused him to move south. In January 1986 he became one of the founder members of a new daily paper, The Racing Post, where he is currently an associate editor.

Along the way, his working field of vision has gradually moved away from what happens on the course, and has become more concentrated on the racing industry's corridors of power and the general "political" scene in racing. He has been a member of the BHB's Flat Racing Committee since 1986 and is President of the Doncaster Racecourse Annual Members' Committee since 2002. He lives near Epsom, having swapped residence near the home of one of the great Classic races for another. In 2004 he became the Vice Chair of the SYTT that runs the NRC.

Howard Wright with Darasin at Rossington Hall

Sadly that same year 2004 saw the untimely death of Lord Scarbrough, the NRC President, who had regularly attended Board meetings during the 18 years he had held the post. His racing colours of light blue and white stripes are preserved in a glass frame in the tack room as a reminder of all the help he gave the College, especially after he became the Lord Lieutenant of South Yorkshire in 1996. As a tribute to the man every seat and pew was filled at his funeral service held at Sheffield Cathedral and, although the NRC was represented, there were many who would have liked to be there who could not be accommodated. In April 2005, the Duke of Devonshire, known to his associates as "Stoker", who had long been a supporter of the College, and was as important a figure in the horseracing industry as anyone in Britain, agreed to become the second President of the NRC.

Triple Accolades in 2006

For four days in May 2006, a team of four inspectors from the Adult Learning Inspectorate trawled all over the NRC, looking at every aspect of the College's training programme and organisation. Twenty-three members of staff were interviewed, while two of the Inspectors concentrated on the work-based provision out in the trainers' yards visiting twelve centres. One Inspector devoted his time solely to assessing leadership and management and was impressed with what he saw of the staff's vision and their pursuit of the business objectives of the College. This time the NRC was given a resounding vote of approval, and was awarded the top grade of "Outstanding". It was a most satisfactory way for the College to celebrate twenty years of existence as an independent trust, and the final report could not have been more complimentary if the staff had written it themselves.

The ALI report said; *"The overall effectiveness of the provision is outstanding. The leadership and management is outstanding, as are its arrangements for quality improvement."*

"The organisation is self-critical and there is a strong commitment to improving its performance and achievement, and retention rates show a marked improvement over the last three years. The NRC has taken action to deal with weaknesses from the previous inspection as well as developing its strengths."

The Inspectors drew attention to the high achievement rates at NVQ Level 1, where over 90% of trainees have been successful since 2002, equating to 100 trainees each year, and they were impressed that 95% of the 2005 intake had now gone on to paid employment in the industry. When the Inspectors asked the trainees (and forty-five trainees were interviewed) what they particularly liked about the NRC, they responded; *"the whole package."*

As if this report was not good enough, David Sherlock, the Chief Inspector, when speaking at the launch of his 2005-6 Report, singled out the NRC, and also the BRS, as

The Board of Management of the South Yorkshire Training Trust
June 2007

Back Row L to R: Jim Gale; Sandra Golding (Senior Admin.Officer); Mike Mason; Howard Wright (V-Chair); Steve Astaire; Alison Harris; Chris Mallinson; James Hetherton; Peter Brindley and Paul Foster. Front Row L to R: Colin Wedd (Chair); Sandy Young; Coun. Barry Johnson (DMBC observer) and Tim Lyle. Absent. Graham Orange; Joe Daniels; Sandy Murphy and Stancee Wedd (Friends of NRC observer)

Among the new trustees were Alison Harris, who includes among her other credentials, the Yorkshire Regional Chair of the British Horse Society and, previously, Membership of the National Council of Riding for the Disabled. When Gordon Gallimore retired in December 2004, Chris Mallinson, who is a racehorse owner but had long been a supporter of the NRC, came onto the Board and Mrs. Sandy Murphy, the former Chief Executive of the Amateur Jockeys' Association, joined in April 2005. Finally, in December 2005, James Hetherton, who trains at Malton and is the Chair of the NRC's Trainers' Advisory Committee, joined along with Peter Brindley MBE, the former Chair of Doncaster Strategic Partnership.

being one of the "Best of the Best." He reported that during the year the ALI had carried out 500 inspections of a wide variety of training institutions and only 151 were regarded as "Outstanding Achievers". Within this group, only 18, including the NRC, had achieved the top grade for every aspect of their training and could be considered the "Best of the Best".

Mark Whitefield

Mark was born and brought up in Doncaster. He graduated from the De Montford University, Leicester, in 1992 and then gained a Master's Degree in Information Management from the University of Sheffield in 1993. He joined the NRC as the Quality Manager, with a place on the Management Team in December 2004, after a period in the Chemical and Waste Management industries. He heads a team of three others to support the improvement of quality right across the NRC's operations, as well as preparing submissions and negotiating contracts for funding with bodies like the LSC. He was the NRC's nominee to work with the ALI inspectors in 2006 and played a major part in the preparation of the application for Beacon status in 2007.

To round off a most successful year, the College also achieved ISO9001 Certification, an internationally recognised award that certifies the effectiveness of quality management systems. A considerable amount of the credit for this award, and the ALI grades, goes to Mark Whitefield, the NRC's Quality Manager, who has put in place systems to analyse feedback from the College's stakeholder partners, and to improve the internal verification of assessments and the audit of procedures. It may sound like modern management-speak to outsiders, but the upshot is to focus on improved training standards, to which the College constantly aspires.

At this significant moment in the College's history, Jim Gale moved over and relinquished direct control of the NRC. Working closely with his Chairman, Colin Wedd, Jim has played a massive part in the development of the College since 1982, when he was singled out, almost at random, when working for the former County Council, to investigate whether a racing training school could possibly be a starter in South Yorkshire. His importance to the national development of horse racing training was already recognised in July 2004 when he was invited to a reception at Buckingham Palace for individuals who were judged in their many and varied walks of life to be "Pioneers in Society". He was somewhat surprised to be invited, and even more surprised to find he was in the close company of Margaret Thatcher and Cliff Richard. He remains as the Chief Executive of the overall operations of the SYTT, and will now have more time to concentrate on the St. Leger Horse and Country Park which is the next big project for the Trust, now that the NRC is so clearly running successfully and confident about its expanding future.

Setting the Pace

The Future – Post 2007

After almost a quarter of a century, the Northern Racing College could afford to take a "rest in the saddle" and consolidate what it has achieved. With a revenue budget of £1.3 million (almost half of it, £616,000, staffing costs) it could have calmly allowed the pace of change to be dictated by external changes, such as Government legislation or new racing industry regulations and training requirements. In the past it was easier for successful institutions to sit in the "comfort zone" on the plateau of their own achievements and decide at leisure how, or if, they would progress. The pace of accelerating change in the modern world makes such complacency a luxury, except perhaps for a lucky few, as the global economy can suddenly render you obsolete as new and better processes and systems are devised in places you may never have heard of.

There was no chance that the NRC and the Trust would look to stand still in the future. However, apart from new ideas for advancing their core activity, the racing training college, they have the advantage of opportunities not often available to most institutions and, clearly, among the most exciting developments for the future is the evolution of the St. Leger Horse and Country Park. That would not have been a possibility if the NRC had not, fortuitously, started their operations in such a small way in the corner of the stables of a former country house, surrounded by a traditional country estate. Nor could the Trust foresee that the 2012 Olympics would come to Britain (we all, including Tony Blair, expected Paris to be selected), and that this huge international event could provide exciting opportunities for the NRC.

The NRC itself is already expanding the range of courses it now offers and this will continue, especially in respect of courses for jockeys and other specialist racing staff. Possibilities include short refresher courses for older riders who need to know modern techniques, perhaps to kick start their careers, and a Jockeys' Academy, where at the other end of the age range, promising youngsters selected by NRC staff from among their trainees, would undertake a specialist course to start their careers as jockeys. Racing needs to develop the Academy concept, which has improved standards in other sports, e.g. Cricket (at least in Australia), Football and Rugby League. It will also help to offset the shortage of top British jockeys who will be better able to challenge foreign riders, especially the numerous successful Irish jockeys. In the new Visitor Centre there may be a remedial centre for injured jockeys, as well as a Fitness Suite for those on current Foundation Courses and a revived P.E. programme for trainees.

One of the simulators in their new venue. Brian Watson, one of the training instructors, is seen putting his "horse" through its paces.

Among the planned new projects is one to develop the scope of the training offered by the two horse simulators, one of which the College has owned since 1993. They were recently moved into the extreme west wing of the Victorian Stables, underneath the classroom, where they are mounted side by side in a dedicated room sponsored by Northern Racing, a company run by twelve racecourses. Surrounded by large photos of several English courses, the plan is to have the "horses" facing a large screen so that different racecourses, including Newcastle, Fontwell, Sedgefield and Hexham can be projected onto the screen in front of the riders. Trainees "riding" on the simulators will then be able to familiarise themselves with these courses and learn how to approach different sections of each course. Today's trainees, familiar with playstations and video games, may not find the technology as amazing as the older generation, but it is an impressive addition to the training resources, especially when the simulator is in full gallop mode. To complete the race meeting atmosphere the large red weighing scales, that did service for many years weighing jockeys at Doncaster Racecourse, stands guard by the entrance to the room.

The New Visitor Centre

The Visitor Centre, an extension to the Indoor Riding School, will be the next building project to be completed, when it is finished at the end of 2007. Costing £660,000, it will be financed with a grant of £270, 000 from an Objective One Rural Growth Enterprise Grant, funded equally from European Money and from the Government Department, DEFRA. The remainder of the money will be found from a £60,000 contribution from the Levy Board, the SYTT's own development funds and from a bank loan from Weatherbys Bank. Togel

The College is delighted to provide a home for the old weighing scales that did such good service weighing jockeys at Doncaster racecourse over the years. Included in the picture are some of the NRC's training instructors. From left to right they are Brian Watson, Malcolm Bygrave, Dave Griffiths, Ray Petersen and Emma Smith.

Construction of Doncaster started on site in July 2007 and the finished building will include a conference room/lecture theatre, where the NRC hopes to host large, even international, equine conferences, and other training facilities, as well as a cafeteria and a souvenir shop. A two-storey building, designed by Building Link Design of Doncaster, the new centre will, as the name implies, be the first point of call for visitors and is well situated, half way along the entrance drive, to act as the reception point for the Country Park

In the 2002 Master Plan for the Country Park it was envisaged that the Visitor Centre would be in the Victorian Stables, with a souvenir shop, a museum and a café, with additional tables set up in the yard as an outdoor eating area. In some ways it was an obvious choice, bringing people right into the heart of the complex and greeting them at the most handsome structure on site. However, the Trust decided, partly because of the high cost of conversion, that the Victorian Stables had a more important role as the heart of the training activities of the NRC and so the Visitor Centre is to be built adjoining the Indoor Riding School.

The immediate capital programme for the Trust is estimated at £1.2 million, with a stable complex attached to the Indoor Riding School and more residential units planned for the woodland area behind the Victorian Stables. By the summer of 2009 it is hoped that there will be a new stable complex in the Hay Barn, not far from the Visitor Centre, with a referral centre run by a York based Veterinary Hospital. There, the vets will have an office and run a clinic, with x-ray facilities and the capacity to perform small operations, for horses in the Doncaster area. Because of the use of haylage, there is not the same demand for storage space for hay as previously, so the Hay Barn's original purpose has been modified to allow extra stable space. This new facility will allow increased commercial use of the complex for livery services, breeding from NRC's mares and stallion, and trekking for visitors who just want the opportunity to sit on a moving horse, preferably at walking pace.

St. Leger Horse and Country Park

From the earliest days at Rossington Hall, the Trust could see the potential of the whole of the site adjacent to the College, with the great country house and its surrounding estate. But it could only be a dream as the Chairman, Chief Executive, Trustees and Staff first concentrated on the sheer logistics of survival, and then on a period of gradual development of their own NRC facilities. By 2000 the SYTT had enough confidence to start to think seriously about what else they could achieve on the site, if it was financially possible and the land and buildings became available. No-one had their imagination more fired up by the potential of the estate than Jim Gale, who saw the development of a Country Park as the obvious, dramatic and stimulating way forward for the Trust and for the NRC. Some trustees were cautious about the idea, perhaps fearing that the "child" might swallow up its "parent", but they agreed to a consultant's report and that was presented by RMJM in 2002.

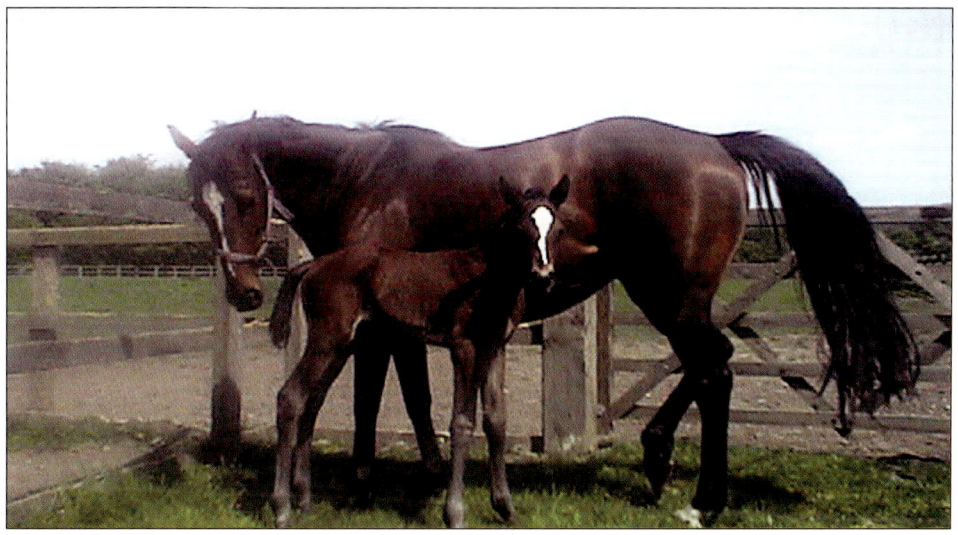

Also the future!
One of the College's mares with her foal at Rossington Hall.

This report was more than a survey of the recreational possibilities of the site, but rather it sought to put the recreation aspects into the wider context of green issues and a sustainable landscape. First and foremost their vision was to create a centre of excellence for horseracing training and education, within a very pleasant and comfortable environment. However, they wanted to link the NRC's successful continuum with the development of a general equestrian centre. They wrote in their introduction;

> *"Within the role of education is also the need to extend the Rossington Hall experience so that the general public can appreciate the sights, sounds and smells of living and working with horses."*

They reckoned that in an urban country like Britain, there were many thousands who would welcome the chance to see and enjoy close contact with horses. This was something townspeople knew about but rarely experienced, unlike their grandparents, for whom the sight of horses was still commonplace in their youth, even if they lived in industrial cities. People would be able to reconnect with their own heritage, which the technology of the twentieth century has taken away from them. At the same time the report indicated that, like the country estate of Rossington Hall in the 19th Century, the Country Park should be a self-sufficient working landscape;

> *"The underlying principles of the 'Masterplan' proposal is that the equestrian country park grows out of a sustainable landscape. It requires a new look at the site in terms of its resources. The new build will be based on energy efficient principles."*

These include, the report stressed, natural ventilation and thermal insulation to create energy efficient buildings, getting an energy supply from the land, and developing the use of alternative sources of energy. Water conservation – likely to be one of the planet's biggest, future issues – could be addressed by implementation of a "grey" water system to flush toilets, rainwater for irrigation, reedbeds for waste-water management, including the stables run-off. Furthermore, they stressed that those managing the Country Park, should in the future recycle materials where possible and increase the bio-diversity of the site by use of native species.

One part of the "Masterplan" that is already in place is the new, six furlong, gallop which was constructed by a local farm contractor with the help of NRC staff and students in 2006. In fact it is two parallel gallops, one of wood chip and the other grass, which run across the additional 55 acres (22 hectares) of land that the Trust have acquired under the terms of an agricultural tenancy in order to develop the Country Park. Jim Gale is particularly keen to resurrect the Italian Garden, the main feature of the Hall's Victorian gardens, now lying dormant under weeds, nettles and scrub but which could once again become a beautiful feature of the grounds of the Hall. Described by one famous Italian landscape architect, Mauro Cempa, as one of the finest Italian gardens in Europe, it could be a major visitor attraction in its own right, like the Japanese gardens at the Irish

The St. Leger Eco Project

SYTT have adopted an Environmental Policy and, in line with it, the Board have backed a recent proposal from John Harris, a long-time Friend of the NRC, who was the Chief Executive of the South Yorkshire County Council when the College was first established in 1984. He chairs a working party to promote the creation of a "St. Leger Carbon Saving and Offsetting Project" to raise money for investment, through grants and by companies and individuals, in the sustainable development on site, which will help to reduce and offset the carbon emissions of the local economy and the surrounding community. He had become much more aware of the serious impact of climate change during his eight-year period as the Chair of the Coal Authority (the privatisation successor to the NCB) and here was an opportunity to do something positive to redress the damage to the environment. 3,000 trees had already been planted in the Country Park in Spring 2007 and this was only part funded by grants. The potential is for thousands of trees, plus new hedges and coppicing, to be planted in the Park. The top priority for 2007 is to install green sources of energy in the new visitor centre and the adjoining riding school. Working in conjunction with Yorkshire Micro-generation a series of projects are being identified throughout the NRC's operations and buildings, as well as in the Country Park. The project would also encourage and support all the other "green" initiatives that were also part of the thinking in the "Masterplan", and would actively encourage working with local partners in Rossington and further afield, to widen the scope of the project.

National Stud at Kildare. Attached to the Hall, there is a splendid walled garden that could be an attractive haven for future visitors, and the whole complex could become as well known as the gardens of Constable Burton or Hardwick Hall.

The Trust has to be sure that, after a major investment in the Country Park, it will actually attract enough visitors to make it viable. There are at least two classic cautionary tales in South Yorkshire of projects that crashed despite the enthusiasm of their founders. Neither the Earth Centre at Denaby, nor the National Popular Music Centre in central Sheffield, had enough appeal to encourage people to come in numbers and, perhaps more important, return for subsequent visits. However, there are six million people within one hour's driving time of Rossington Hall, and Yorkshire is a sporting county par excellence, (there are 700,000 active sportsmen and women within Yorkshire, with half of them members of sports clubs,) and it is a hard bitten county that demands the best of performance and facilities in sport.

Doncaster MBC has decided to close the school at Rossington Hall, and that opens up the possibility for the Trust to have the opportunity to expend in other directions. One

Seven trainees who helped to create the new gallop take a well-earned rest from their labours. Left to right they are; Lianne Bridson, Emma Stanley, Sophie Young, Alice Hewitt, Phillipa Scott, Vanessa Robb and Jordan Mullaney.Unfortunately the severe floods, which devastated several areas of Doncaster in June 2007, washed away a third of the gallop and it will have to be re-laid.

suggestion from the consultants was that it could become a land-based sector college, a South Yorkshire equivalent of Bishop Burton College, with a heavy emphasis on equine studies such as are currently carried out at that East Riding college.

The models for some of these ideas are the Kentucky Horse Park, which is a working farm of 1200 acres, in the "Bluegrass" State near Lexington, which includes two museums, twin theatres and fifty different breeds of horse. The St. Leger Horse and Country Park might also house a Museum of the Horse in an enlarged Visitor Centre, such as the one at Newmarket that attracts 27,000 visitors annually. San Rossare, near Pisa, which is much more familiar to the NRC, is another example of what can be achieved on a larger site. They have a racecourse, a training school and other equine facilities within a large complex known as the "Village of the Horse." Other ideas may come from the Rhineland Equitation College near Cologne, which includes training in Show Jumping, Dressage and Three Day Eventing, some of which the NRC does offer already.

For some time there have been Polo-Crosse matches, where the ball is passed and propelled as in Lacrosse, and the European Championships were held at Rosington Hall in 2006 and 2007, and the British team, who were the runners up in the World

Trainees are introduced to the Starting Stalls at Rossington Hall. Will they be the top jockeys of the future?

Championships, trained there before flying out to Australia for the 2007 event. Show Jumping and Dressage, both indoor and outdoor, feature regularly and the Doncaster Show Jumping Association hold their annual three-day event at Rossington Hall every year. In the Twenties there was an international cross-country course at Rossington Hall, and this could be redesigned and restored, and one cannot rule out the possibility of Polo being played in the restored grounds in the future. There could well be a major national horse event that included every aspect of equine life, along the lines of the "Pageant Of the Horse", which was such a success when the former South Yorkshire County Council ran it for many years at Doncaster Racecourse. It would all add to the critical mass of the equestrian activity and education on the site, and yet be available to the casual visitor who just enjoys a day at an attractive country location and observing horses undertaking different activities.

Within the St Leger Horse and Country Park in the future there will be room for many more activities, some of which may be contracted out by NRC Trading Limited, who will probably manage the Park, collecting the rent and keeping a landlord's eye on its tenants. The catering and retailing outlet will probably be handled this way, and any future capacity for livery service will be rented out, as the Trust's experience of running a livery service itself is that it is very time consuming and fraught with petty difficulties. It has all been described as a jigsaw approach to fitting in new facilities and activities, with private contractors bidding for options within the NRC's overall strategy and control.

The NRC and the 2012 Olympic Games

The NRC was quick off the mark to offer its facilities once it was announced in Singapore, in 2005, that Britain was awarded the 2012 Olympics. A first class equestrian training centre has a great deal to offer the Games' organisers, who will need facilities for competing national equestrian teams to train in British conditions in the period running up to the Olympiad. Ben Mico leads for the College in discussions within a steering group representing a consortium of twenty-nine facilities in South Yorkshire, which include some of the best facilities for athletics, swimming and diving anywhere in Europe. Some of the major nations competing in the equestrian sports may want to set up training camps as much as three years before the event, and Rossington Hall seems well placed to accommodate them. The possibility of having world class show jumpers, dressage and cross-country riders on site before and during the Games is very exciting, especially for young trainees coming into the industry. It also, of course, offers an ideal opportunity for marketing the College and the Country Park as a prestigious venue. No decisions have yet been made, but the NRC has passed through the first of the three levels of submissions, and is confident that it will get a chance to play a part in the Olympics when they come to Britain.

Dream Plans

If Harry Lindley had a dream of a racing training school back in 1982, then the people currently in charge at Rossington Hall have a new dream that is just as bold. Harry's dream came true, and he would be truly amazed at the success and extent of the College today. In May 2007 the NRC picked up another prestigious award, when it was confirmed as a training institution with Beacon Status, an award made by the Government's own DfES Quality Improvement Agency, which could benefit the NRC with financial support for agreed projects over the next few years.

In the new dream, the NRC continues to progress while the Trust develops the surrounding area, creates the Country Park, links with regeneration work being done in Rossington village, and plays as full a part as possible in Doncaster's aspirations to be a city at the heart of a thriving sub-region, with one of the fastest growing economies in the U.K. The Park may attract up to 150,000 visitors when it is finally in operation, but the Trust also intends to expand its role in developing the green areas to the west, across the main railway line that links London to the North East and Scotland. Here is planned a landscape of parkland, woods and heathland, where the bridlepaths, cycleways and footpaths that start at Rossington Hall can continue into the valley of the River Torne and bring added enjoyment and recreational opportunities. All this will enhance the countryside around Rossington itself, providing an important part of the regeneration of the former pit village. Finally, the proximity of Robin Hood Airport, only one mile to the east at nearby Finningley, may also produce a synergy of ideas and advantages for the SYTT, the Country Park, the NRC and the local community.

Doncaster is in a strong position to benefit from a unique confluence of circumstances. It has excellent road, rail and air links (already racehorses, including the 2006 St. Leger winner, are being flown into the new airport to take part in races in the town and the region) along with its racing heritage and the growing cluster of equine activities in the locality. Jim Gale is promoting the idea that, with some joined-up town and country planning, the regeneration of Rossington should become an "Eco-town", marketing itself as the "airport town" as well as being ideally placed to be an inland port transferring freight between rail, road and air. An extended eco-friendly St. Leger Horse and Country Park would wrap itself around Rossington and ensure the NRC was outward looking and a major player in the all the exciting new developments planned for its neighbourhood.

This new vision is being driven by Colin Wedd and Jim Gale, who can make a fair claim to be regarded as the "Founding Fathers" of the NRC. In 1984 they led the first tentative steps taken by the new racing training school, when they were motivated as much by concern about youth unemployment as they were about the needs of the racing industry. Colin Wedd recognising the vital economic importance of the horseracing "industry" to the nation, commented recently; *the relationship of humans to horses is something very special, whether it is working with horses or just watching them perform. We want to see at Rossington Hall a beacon of excellence in all matters equestrian, for youngsters to learn, for skills to be improved and for the general public to enjoy, and gain knowledge about, horses and horseracing."*

If past record is anything to go by, new people, in the future, will build on the present achievements at the NRC and take it in positive directions as yet uncharted, thereby achieving the College's vision of being *"the Best Racing College in Europe".*